Pegs to Hang Ideas On

Pegs to Hang Ideas On

A Book of Quotations

selected by Marjorie P. Katz
and Jean S. Arbeiter

M. Evans and Company,
New York

M. Evans and Company titles are distributed in the United States by the J. B. Lippincott, Company, East Washington Square, Philadelphia, Pa. 19105 and in Canada by McClelland & Stewart, Ltd., 25 Hollinger Road, Toronto, 374, Ontario.

Library of Congress Catalog Card Number: 76-187739

ISBN 0-87131-085-6

Designed by Vincent Torre

Manufactured in the United States of America

9 8 7 6 5 4 3 2 1

ACKNOWLEDGMENTS

Some of the quotations in this collection are from works still in copyright. Although the editors understand that properly credited quotation of isolated small excerpts in a reference work, such as found in this volume, constitutes fair use under the copyright laws, they have offered a scale of payment for use of any substantial amount of materials still in copyright in the United States, to which the publishers listed below have graciously agreed as to the works which they control. If any holders of rights have been overlooked, the editors offer their apologies and the promise of correction in later editions as well as payment on the same scale.

Thanks are due to the following authors, publishers, publications and agents for permission to use the material included:

Coward, McCann & Geoghegan, Inc. for two excerpts from *The American Dream* by Edward Albee. Reprinted by permission of Coward, McCann & Geoghegan, Inc. from *The American Dream* by Edward Albee. Copyright © 1960, 1961 by Edward Albee.

Curtis Brown, Ltd. for an excerpt from "What Makes the Sky Blue?" from *The Moon Is Shining Bright as Day* by Ogden Nash. Reprinted by permission of Curtis Brown, Ltd. Copyright © 1953 by Ogden Nash. All rights reserved; for an excerpt from "Hymn to the Thing That Makes the Wolf Go" by Ogden Nash. Reprinted by permission of Curtis Brown, Ltd. Copyright © 1934 by Ogden Nash. All rights reserved.

J. M. Dent & Sons Ltd. for extracts from "A Refusal to Mourn" and "Do Not Go Gentle" from *Collected Poems of Dylan Thomas* by Dylan Thomas. Reprinted by permission of J. M. Dent & Sons Ltd. and the Trustees for the Copyrights of the late Dylan Thomas.

Doubleday & Company, Inc. for excerpts from "Random Thoughts by Archy" from *Archy's Life of Mehitabel* by Don Marquis. Copyright 1933 by Doubleday & Company, Inc. Reprinted by permission of Doubleday & Company, Inc.

Gerald Duckworth & Co., Ltd. for an excerpt from "In the Fields" from *Collected Poems* by Charlotte Mew. Copyright 1953 by Gerald Duckworth & Co., Ltd.

IV

V

VI

For Suzanne and Gilbert Jr.
in memory of their mother and our friend
Jane Geisman Chevalier

All words are pegs to hang ideas on.
Henry Ward Beecher

Contents

Foreword

PEGS TO HANG IDEAS ON is a new kind of book of quotations, compiled with today's young reader in mind. Most traditional compilations do not challenge a student to think on his own; they do not serve as pathways to deeper reflection and other ideas. This is because the quotations are "locked" into categories that are narrow and rigid; the ideas themselves do not flow freely, they cannot be seen in all of their aspects. Thus presented, quotations are useful only for "quoting." Like Polonius' advice to Laertes, certain quotations have become clichés, pronouncements which turn the reader off rather than stimulate him.

   We believe the quotation itself is more important than the person who said it. No selection was made on the basis of feeling the need to represent a particular writer. For this book we went to contemporary newspapers and magazines, searching out the words of public figures ranging from sports heroes and rock stars to statesmen and university professors; we went to traditional children's literature; and we pored over a multitude of familiar, adult-oriented works, analyzing thousands of words to uncover those that would speak to today's students, communicating to them important ideas about their world. For many, these capsules will be an introduction to the thinking of those who have changed our way of looking at our world or, indeed, have changed our world itself.

We have organized this volume into categories which are both open and life-related. They flow easily into one another. They are suggestive rather than binding. Each category leads readily to another and to making connections between ideas. The categories relate to the reader's personal development, his environment and his world, and his confrontation with the major social and political questions of our times.

All ideas can be contemporary; the relevance of an idea has little to do with the time when it was written. In some traditional and predictable sources we have discovered some refreshingly unpredictable excerpts. But we have also included several familiar quotations, placing them in new company so that they may be read with new insights. We have tried to achieve a purposeful juxtaposition of quotations within a category to contrast ideas voiced in different times or places, to present expressions of different points of view, or to show several expressions of similar or related ideas.

We hope we have created a book that can be browsed through with enjoyment, a book in which the reader will find new ideas to consider, some to accept, some to reject. Perhaps he will come across a thought that parallels his own. We hope his understanding of his world will grow as he measures it against the thoughts and perceptions of others.

Marjorie P. Katz
Jean S. Arbeiter
1973

I

"A Shaft of Sunlight at the End of a Dark Afternoon"

1. Things That Really Count

"Henry Rackmeyer, you tell us what is important."
"A shaft of sunlight at the end of a dark afternoon, a
note in music, and the way the back of a baby's neck
smells if its mother keeps it tidy," answered Henry.
"Correct," said Stuart. "Those are the important
things."

E. B. WHITE
Stuart Little

The significance of man is not in what he attains, but
rather in what he longs to attain.

KAHLIL GIBRAN

All of the animals, excepting man, know that the
principal business of life is to enjoy it.

SAMUEL BUTLER

Happy Birthday, Johnny,
Live beyond your income,
Travel for enjoyment,
Follow your own nose.

W. H. AUDEN
"Many Happy Returns"

I was hungered, and ye gave me meat: I was thirsty,
and ye gave me drink: I was a stranger, and ye took
me in.

MATTHEW 25:35

What is life but a series of inspired follies? The
difficulty is to find them to do. Never lose a chance:
it doesn't come every day.

GEORGE BERNARD SHAW

And now here is my secret, a very simple secret:
It is only with the heart that one can see rightly; what
is essential is invisible to the eye.

ANTOINE DE SAINT-EXUPÉRY
The Little Prince

What counts is not the best living but the most living.

ALBERT CAMUS
The Myth of Sisyphus

I know a planet where there is a certain red-faced
gentleman. He has never smelled a flower. He has
never looked at a star. He has never loved anyone.
He has never done anything in his life but add up
figures. And all day he says over and over . . . "I am
busy with matters of consequence." And that makes
him swell up with pride. But he is not a man—he is
a mushroom!

ANTOINE DE SAINT-EXUPÉRY
The Little Prince

The one thing in the world of value, is the active
soul,—the soul, free, sovereign, active. This every man
is entitled to; this every man contains within him,
although in almost all men, obstructed, and as yet

unborn. The soul active sees absolute truth; and utters truth, or creates.

RALPH WALDO EMERSON
American Scholar, *1837*

━━━━━━━

Act as if you were going to live forever and cast your plan way ahead. If your contributions have been vital, there will always be somebody to pick up where you left off, and that will be your claim to immortality.

WALTER GROPIUS
recalled after his death,
The New York Times, *July 7, 1969*

━━━━━━━

Every artist wants his work to be permanent. But what is? The Aswan Dam covered some of the greatest art in the world. Venice is sinking. Great books and pictures were lost in the Florence floods. In the meantime we still enjoy butterflies.

ROMARE BEARDON
New York Post, *August 5, 1972*

━━━━━━━

Life is absolutely super and wonderful. There shouldn't be any sadness in it. People should be aware of all things at all times, they should experience the extremities of life, fulfill themselves completely. Why does everyone want to go to sleep when the only thing left is to stay awake?

EDWARD ALBEE
The New York Times, *April 18, 1971*

━━━━━━━

As reverence for property has diminished, youth have come to value the intrinsic worth of human relationships. There is an emphasis on being rather than doing. Youth are preoccupied with the need for being good people who can form good relationships ... A "beautiful" person, in the vernacular of today's youth, is not one who is physically attractive or one who has the personal qualities that guarantee success. He is an individual who has the capacity to relate openly and warmly with others.

SEYMOUR L. HALLECK
"Why They'd Rather Do Their Own Thing,"
Think *Magazine, 1968*

We listen too much to the telephone and we listen too little to nature. The wind is one of my sounds. A lonely sound, perhaps, but soothing. Everybody should have his personal sounds to listen for—sounds that will make him exhilarated and alive, or quiet and calm. ... As a matter of fact, one of the greatest sounds of them all— and to me it is a sound—is utter complete silence.

ANDRÉ KOSTELANETZ
New York Journal-American, *February 8, 1955*

If one by one we counted people out
For the least sin, it wouldn't take us long
To get so we had no one left to live with.
For to be social is to be forgiving.

ROBERT FROST
"The Star-Splitter"

The last time I glanced at the library books on the kitchen shelf they were more than five months overdue, and I wondered whether I would have chosen differently if I had known that these were the last books, the ones which would stand forever on our kitchen shelf.

SHIRLEY JACKSON
We Have Always Lived in the Castle

Just as Adam was put in the Garden of Eden to dress it, we are here to look after the universe. By that I think that one has to help the universe realize goals which it cannot realize itself.

W. H. AUDEN
The New York Times, *February 2, 1971*

You cannot believe in honor until you have achieved it. Better keep yourself clean and bright: you are the window through which you must see the world.

GEORGE BERNARD SHAW
Maxims for Revolutionists

I had a question and it was the age-old one about whether or not you sell your birthright.
"Mr. Rickey," I asked, "are you looking for a Negro who is afraid to fight back?"
I'll never forget the way he exploded.
"Robinson," he said, "I'm looking for a ballplayer with guts enough not to fight back."

JACKIE ROBINSON
I Never Had It Made

There is only one success—to be able to spend your life in your own way.

CHRISTOPHER MORLEY
Where the Blue Begins

There is nothing—absolutely nothing—half so much worth doing as simply messing about in boats.

KENNETH GRAHAME
The Wind in the Willows

But not only medicine, engineering, and painting are arts; *living itself is an art*—in fact, the most important and at the same time the most difficult and complex art to be practiced by man.

ERICH FROMM
Man For Himself

Supposing a man from another planet who had never seen a flower and he was shown a flower—he could say—"I don't know what it is—but OH I LIKE IT"—

JOHN MARIN
John Marin on John Marin

6

A child's world is fresh and new and beautiful, full of wonder and excitement. It is our misfortune that for most of us that clear-eyed vision, that true instinct for what is beautiful and awe-inspiring, is dimmed and even lost before we reach adulthood. If I had influence with the good fairy who is supposed to preside over the christening of all children I should ask that her gift to each child in the world be a sense of wonder so indestructible that it would last throughout life, as an unfailing antidote against the boredom and disenchantments of later years, the sterile preoccupation with things that are artificial, the alienation from the sources of our strength.

RACHEL CARSON
The Sense of Wonder

A nation declines when its people become too serious to set their hearts on toys.

ERIC HOFFER
The New York Times Magazine, *April 25, 1971*

II

"Are We to Have a Chance to Live?"

2. Progress, Technology and the Future

Are we to have a chance to live? We don't ask for prosperity, or security. Only for a reasonable chance to live, to work out our destiny in peace and decency. Not to go down in history as the apocalyptic generation.

GEORGE WALD
"A Generation in Search of a Future,"
The New Yorker, *March 22, 1969*

The future is of our own making—and (for me) the most striking characteristic of the century is just that development.

JOSEPH CONRAD
Letter to H. G. Wells, *1903*

... Perhaps we foresee a time when men, exultant in the technique of homicide, will rage so hotly over the world that every precious thing will be in danger, every book and picture and harmony, every treasure garnered through two millenniums, the small, the delicate, the defenseless—all will be lost or wrecked or utterly destroyed.

JAMES HILTON
Lost Horizon

The really great lessons of that experiment, however, belong to no special group but to all mankind. The

atomic era, fortunately or otherwise, is now man's
environment, to control or to adapt himself to as he can.

DAVID BRADLEY
No Place to Hide

We may define future shock as the distress, both
physical and psychological, that arises from an overload
of the human organism's physical adaptive systems
and its decision-making processes. Put more simply,
future shock is the human response to overstimulation.

ALVIN TOFFLER
Future Shock

Progress, therefore, is not an accident, but a necessity.
. . . It is a part of nature.

HERBERT SPENCER
Social Statics

There are discoverable limits to the amount of change
that the human organism can absorb . . .

ALVIN TOFFLER
Future Shock

The automobile has become such an important
member of the American family that many of us house
and clean our cars and worry about their health almost
as if they were alive.

THE AMERICAN MUSEUM OF NATURAL HISTORY, NEW YORK
Handbook to exhibit Can Man Survive?, 1969

The farm house lingers, though averse to square
With the new city street it has to wear
A number in.

ROBERT FROST
"A Brook in the City"

11

An epoch will come when people will disclaim kinship
with us as we disclaim kinship with the monkeys.

KAHLIL GIBRAN

The power that produced Man when the monkey was
not up to the mark, can produce a higher creature than
Man if Man does not come up to the mark.

GEORGE BERNARD SHAW
Preface, Back to Methuselah

I like the dreams of the future better than the history
of the past.

THOMAS JEFFERSON
Letter to John Adams, *August 1, 1816*

If the future is to remain open and free, we have to
rear individuals who can tolerate the unknown, who
will not need the support of completely worked-out
systems, whether they be traditional ones from the past
or blueprints of the future.

MARGARET MEAD
New Lives for Old

Would you realize what Revolution is, call it Progress;
and would you realize what Progress is, call it Tomorrow.

VICTOR HUGO
Les Misérables

You can't say that civilization don't advance, for in
every war they kill you in a new way.

WILL ROGERS
Autobiography

At the end of the first half-century of engine-driven
flight, we are confronted with the stark fact that the

12

historical significance of aircraft has been primarily
military and destructive.

CHARLES A. LINDBERGH
The New York Times, *February 2, 1954*

Society produces technology and technology produces
society in an endless mesh of action and interaction.

KENNETH E. BOULDING
"Technology and the Changing Social Order"
in The Urban-Industrial Frontier

Today's children are the first generation to grow up in
a world that has the power to destroy itself.

MARGARET MEAD
A Way of Seeing

And what rough beast, its hour come round at last,
Slouches towards Bethlehem to be born?

WILLIAM BUTLER YEATS
"The Second Coming"

The next great step of mankind is to step into the
nature of his own mind.

STANLEY KAUFFMAN
A World on Film

This I know. This I believe with all my heart. If we
want a free and peaceful world, if we want to make
deserts bloom and man grow to greater dignity as a
human being—*we can do it!*

ELEANOR ROOSEVELT
in Eleanor: The Years Alone
by Joseph P. Lash

13

3. Revolution and Social Change

I hold it, that a little rebellion, now and then, is a
good thing, and as necessary in the political world as
storms in the physical.

THOMAS JEFFERSON
Letter to James Madison, *January 30, 1787*

The real meaning of revolution is not a change in
management, but a change in man. This change we must
make in our own lifetime and not for our children's
sake, for the revolution must be born of joy and not
sacrifice.

DANIEL COHN-BENDIT
Obsolete Communism, a Left-Wing Alternative

A revolution is interesting insofar as it avoids like the
plague the plague it promised to heal.

PHILIP BERRIGAN
The New York Times, *February 4, 1971*

The reasonable man adapts himself to the world;
the unreasonable one persists in trying to adapt the
world to himself. Therefore all progress depends on the
unreasonable man.

GEORGE BERNARD SHAW
Maxims for Revolutionists

Unjust laws exist: shall we be content to obey them,
or shall we endeavor to amend them, and obey them until
we have succeeded, or shall we transgress them at once?
Men generally, under such a government as this, think
that they ought to wait until they have persuaded the
majority to alter them. They think that, if they should
resist, the remedy would be worse than the evil. But it is
the fault of the government itself that the remedy *is* worse
than the evil. *It* makes it worse. Why is it not more apt
to anticipate and provide for reform? Why does it not
cherish its wise minority? Why does it cry and resist
before it is hurt? Why does it not encourage its citizens
to be on the alert to point out its faults, and *do* better than
it would have them? Why does it always crucify Christ,
and excommunicate Copernicus and Luther, and
pronounce Washington and Franklin rebels?

HENRY DAVID THOREAU
Civil Disobedience

Let not him who is houseless pull down the house of
another, but let him work diligently and build one for
himself, thus by example assuring that his own shall be
safe from violence when built.

ABRAHAM LINCOLN
Address to the New York Working Man's
Democratic Republican Association, 1864

Once you could run away from the problems that
seemed to confound and confuse life in the places
where people congregated. You could go back to the
farm and forget the city. You could go off to the colonies
and forget the home country. You could head for the
South Seas. But today the mushroom clouds from atomic
blasts climb into the air not far from Tahiti. Bulldozers
and chain saws roar in the upper Amazon. There is no
place left to hide. If you want a world fit to live in, you
must fight for it now.

RAYMOND F. DASMANN
An Environment Fit For People

15

The world that we must seek is a world in which the creative spirit is alive, in which life is an adventure full of joy and hope, based rather upon the impulse to construct than upon the desire to retain what we possess or to seize what is possessed by others. It must be a world in which affection has free play, in which love is purged of the instinct for domination, in which cruelty and envy have been dispelled by happiness and the unfettered development of all the instincts that build up life and fill it with mental delights. Such a world is possible; it waits only for men to wish to create it.

BERTRAND RUSSELL
Roads to Freedom

Those who make peaceful revolution impossible will make violent revolution inevitable.

JOHN F. KENNEDY

If there is no struggle, there is no progress. Those who profess to favor freedom and yet deprecate agitation, are men who want crops without plowing up the ground, they want rain without thunder and lightning. . . . This struggle may be a moral one, or it may be a physical one, or it may be both moral and physical, but it must be a struggle. Power concedes nothing without a demand.

FREDERICK DOUGLASS

A revolutionist is one who desires to discard the existing social order and try another. . . . Any person under the age of thirty, who, having any knowledge of the existing social order is not a revolutionist, is an inferior.

GEORGE BERNARD SHAW
The Revolutionist's Handbook

We know through painful experience that freedom is never voluntarily given by the oppressor; it must be

demanded by the oppressed. Frankly, I have yet to
engage in a direct-action campaign that was "well-timed"
in the view of those who have not suffered unduly from
the disease of segregation. For years now I have heard
the word "Wait!" It rings in the ear of every Negro with
piercing familiarity. This "Wait" has almost always
meant "Never."

MARTIN LUTHER KING, JR.
Why We Can't Wait

. . . When your stomach is empty and your mind is full,
it's always hard to sleep.

E. B. WHITE
Charlotte's Web

If the injustice is part of the necessary friction of the
machine of government, let it go, let it go: perchance it
will wear smooth—certainly the machine will wear out.
If the injustice has a spring, or a pulley, or a rope, or a
crank, exclusively for itself, then perhaps you will
consider whether the remedy will not be worse than the
evil; but if it is of such a nature that it requires you to be
the agent of injustice to another, then, I say, break the
law. Let your life be a counter friction to stop the machine.
What I have to do is to see, at any rate, that I do not lend
myself to the wrong which I condemn.

HENRY DAVID THOREAU
Civil Disobedience

Political revolution leads people into support for other
revolutions rather than having them get involved in
making their own. Cultural revolution requires people to
change the way they live and act in the revolution
rather than passing judgments on how the other folks
are proceeding. The cultural view creates outlaws,
politics breeds organizers.

ABBIE HOFFMAN
Woodstock Nation

17

People are always blaming their circumstances for what they are. I don't believe in circumstances. The people who get on in this world are the people who get up and look for the circumstances they want, and, if they cant [sic] find them, make them.

GEORGE BERNARD SHAW
Mrs. Warren's Profession

This country, with its institutions, belongs to the people who inhabit it. Whenever they shall grow weary of the existing government they can exercise their constitutional right of amending it, or their revolutionary right to dismember or overthrow it.

ABRAHAM LINCOLN
First Inaugural Address, March 4, 1861

The future cannot be predicted, but futures can be invented. It was man's ability to invent which has made human society what it is.

DENNIS GABOR
Inventing the Future

And discover the Guru in our own hearts. And set forth within the New Wilderness of machine America to explore open spaces of consciousness in Self and fellow Selves. If there be the necessary revolution in America it will come that way. It's up to us older hairs who still have relation with some of the joy of youth to encourage this revolutionary individual search.

ALLEN GINSBERG
"Public Solitude"

But what do We mean by the American Revolution? Do we mean the American War? The Revolution was effected before the War commenced. The Revolution was in the Minds and Hearts of the People.

JOHN ADAMS
Letter, February 13, 1818

18

4. Cities

A city has values as well as slums, excitement as well
as conflict; it has a personality that has not yet been
obliterated by its highways and gas stations; it has a
spirit as well as a set of arteries and a voice that speaks
the hopes as well as the disappointments of its people.

CHARLES ABRAMS
The City Is the Frontier

A great city is that which has the
    greatest men and women,
If it be a few ragged huts it is still
    the greatest city in the whole world.

WALT WHITMAN
"Song of the Broad-Axe," Leaves of Grass

No, it is not a good place to live. You have to look
up to see the sky.

CHIEF DAN GEORGE
asked about his reaction to New York City,
Time, February 15, 1971

Nobody who has read of crime in the streets and
decaying of the inner cities can want to live in the large
cities. Or would opt to work in the city and spend a large
portion of his life commuting to and from his suburban
home as they do in Chicago and New York.

It isn't my kind of life and the people who live it are
not my kind of people.

I love Wisconsin's small towns, the air of the bucolic
that exists just outside of Milwaukee. . . . I worship the
splendor of her lakes, the green of her trees and the
purity of her northern waters.

Wisconsin of the small town halls, the shuttered
country churches, steeples rising on prairie horizons and
barns and silos looming in the Kettle Moraine country.

I visited New York City once and thought I was in a
foreign country.

LARRY VAN GOETHEM
The New York Times, *June 12, 1971*

What makes men want to gather in cities, once
technology has removed the necessity of their doing
so, is partly such a simple, age-old thing as a liking
for companionship and gossip. But it is also—and
perhaps chiefly—a delight in the amenities which the
city alone provides. These include the color and the
variety of life on the street, the unexpectedness with
which things are always happening—the chance
encounter and the "strange and fatal" interview.

AUGUST HECKSCHER
"Government, The Arts, and The City"
in The Urban Industrial Frontier

The only New York image that has permanently
impressed itself on the national mind is that of
Wall Street—a street on which nobody lives. Paris
may be France, London may be England, but New York,
we continue to reassure ourselves, is *not* America.

NATHAN GLAZER and DANIEL PATRICK MOYNIHAN
Beyond the Melting Pot

I went to San Francisco.
I saw the bridges high
Spun across the water
Like cobwebs in the sky.

LANGSTON HUGHES
The Langston Hughes Reader

The soot is the ugliest sight in New York. The sky
looks snatched from the viewer. As though your eyes
have been ripped out of your head. . . . You wait for
the soot to get swallowed up into the sky. For the
sky to be clean.

JULIUS HORWITZ
The Inhabitants

It is in the city that one finds the excitement of modern
life. It is in the city that life pulsates and vibrates; it is
the city life that is attractive and increasingly beckons
young and old alike.

ARTHUR T. NAFTALIN
"The Old City and the Urban-Industrial Frontier"
in The Urban Industrial Frontier

Our civilization is becoming urban, and the advance
into cities is one of the most spectacular social
phenomena of our time. The city has become the frontier.

CHARLES ABRAMS
The City Is the Frontier

As a remedy to life in society, I would suggest the big
city. Nowadays, it is the only desert within our means.

ALBERT CAMUS
Notebooks 1935–1942

Like a city in dreams, the great white capital stretches
along the placid river from Georgetown on the west to
Anacostia on the east. It is a city of temporaries, a city of
just-arriveds and one-visitings, built on the shifting sands
of politics, filled with people passing through.

ALLEN DRURY
Advise and Consent

Through its concentration of physical and cultural
power, the city heightened the tempo of human
intercourse and translated its products into forms that

could be stored and reproduced. Through its monuments, written records, and orderly habits of association, the city enlarged the scope of all human activities, extending them backwards and forwards in time. By means of its storage facilities (buildings, vaults, archives, monuments, tablets, books), the city became capable of transmitting a complex culture from generation to generation, for it marshalled together not only the physical means but the human agents needed to pass on and enlarge this heritage. That remains the greatest of the city's gifts.

LEWIS MUMFORD
The City in History

All cities are mad: but the madness is gallant. All cities are beautiful: but the beauty is grim.

CHRISTOPHER MORLEY
Where the Blue Begins

City life: Millions of people being lonesome together.

HENRY DAVID THOREAU

A city, in its most real sense, is its buildings. Whatever the life, spirit, activity or achievements of the city may be, they are expressed in the mass of asphalt, brick, stone, marble, steel and glass that has accumulated during the city's existence. The structures that its inhabitants have erected for their use and pride—even the buildings that have come and gone—and the way in which those buildings are disposed upon the streets and squares are the source of its personality, its style, and its distinguishing stamp.

ADA LOUISE HUXTABLE
Classic New York

Hog Butcher for the World,
Tool Maker, Stacker of Wheat,

Player with Railroads and the Nation's
    Freight Handler;
Stormy, husky, brawling.
City of the Big Shoulders.

CARL SANDBURG
"Chicago"

In the morning the city
Spreads its wings
Making a song
Of stone that sings.

In the evening the city
Goes to bed
Hanging lights
About its head.

LANGSTON HUGHES
The Langston Hughes Reader

If the city's chaos is part of its planlessness, its contrasts and variety still offer relief from the sameness of suburbia. . . . People still seek escape to the metropolises, crave contrast, look for occasional anonymity, and want to see more people without being seen. . . . If the nation was just one sprawling network of suburbias, it would be a bore.

CHARLES ABRAMS
The City Is the Frontier

The ballet of the good city sidewalk never repeats itself from place to place, and in any one place is always replete with new improvisations.

JANE JACOBS
The Death and Life of Great American Cities

In small settlements everyone knows your affairs. In the city everyone does not—only those you choose

23

to tell will know about you. This is one of the attributes
of cities that is precious to most city people . . .

JANE JACOBS
The Death and Life of Great American Cities

Big cities and countrysides can get along well together.
Big cities need real countryside close by. And countryside—from man's point of view—needs big cities, with
all their diverse opportunities and productivity, so human
beings can be in a position to appreciate the rest of the
natural world instead of to curse it.

JANE JACOBS
The Death and Life of Great American Cities

In the city, where the triumph of numbers is complete,
the technical collaboration between men persists in the
midst of the greatest loneliness and destructiveness.
There is a meticulous unending confrontation between
man and other men, between man and his *things,*
even between things and *their* things.

ALFRED KAZIN
Introduction to Seize the Day *by Saul Bellow*

That enfabled rock, that ship of life, that swarming
million-footed, tower-masted, and sky-soaring citadel
that bears the magic name of the Island of Manhattan.

THOMAS WOLFE
The Web and the Rock

III

"I Could Understand... By Becoming Myself"

5. Men, Fathers

... I entered the Army, continuing at the same time
my separation from my father and my education toward
him. I could make myself possible by denying him.
I could understand him by becoming myself. I could
enter his soul, if one enters the soul of another, by
suffering his pains. And then I would need defiance
of him no longer.

HERBERT GOLD
Fathers

The man that I remember was an educated soul,
though I think now, looking back, that it was as much
a matter of the physical bearing of my father as his
command of information and of thought that left that
impression upon me.... He carried his head in such a
way that I was quite certain that there was nothing he
was afraid of. Even writing this, how profoundly it
shocks my inner senses to realize suddenly that *my
father*, like all men, must have known *fear*.

LORRAINE HANSBERRY
in To Be Young, Gifted and Black

Oh, Daddy is clever, he's a clever sort of man.

Oh, Daddy is Daddy, he's a Daddy sort of man.

Well, I'm very fond of Daddy, but he hasn't time to play ...

A. A. MILNE
"Binker," Now We Are Six

But the expression of a well-made man appears not only
    in his face,
It is in his limbs and joints also, it is curiously in the joints
    of his hips and wrists,
It is in his walk, the carriage of his neck, the flex of his
    waist and knees, dress does not hide him,
The strong sweet quality he has strikes through the cotton
    and broadcloth,
To see him pass conveys as much as the best poem,
    perhaps more,
You linger to see his back, and the back of his neck and
    shoulder-side.

WALT WHITMAN
"I Sing The Body Electric," Leaves of Grass

We seem to have a great nostalgia for the good old
days —"when men were men"— or so we think. I think
we have greatly romanticized this picture. It was so much
easier for a man to *look* masculine when women were
subservient. A man didn't have to be a real man at all,
and he could fool everybody, including himself. . . .
He played a role, and no one ever really knew or thought
about what he was or felt beneath the surface of that role.

EDA LE SHAN
How to Survive Parenthood

Traditionally the masculine has been the hard and
the militant. But traditions change; in the new atomic
conditions of life, war is not an ultimate test of power
and skill but of self-destruction and madness. This may
conspire with other forces such as coeducation, increasing
sexual freedom, the affluence of the young, the greater
catholicism of more-travelled populations, and the very
media of communication to promote changes in
conceptions of maleness.

LIONEL TIGER
Men in Groups

Manliness is not all swagger and swearing and mountain climbing. Manliness is also tenderness, gentleness, consideration.

ROBERT ANDERSON
Tea and Sympathy

Men are of two kinds, and he
Was of the kind I'd like to be.
Some preach their virtues, and a few
Express their lives by what they do.
That sort was he.

EDGAR A. GUEST
"A Real Man"

Men have a much better time of it than women. For one thing, they marry later. For another thing, they die earlier.

H. L. MENCKEN
A Mencken Chrestomathy

There must always be a struggle between a father and son, while one aims at power and the other at independence.

SAMUEL JOHNSON
in Boswell's Life of Samuel Johnson,
July 4, 1763

'Tis strange what a man may do, and a woman yet think him an angel.

WILLIAM MAKEPEACE THACKERAY
Henry Esmond

To be fully male or fully female means to be paternal or maternal. Animals are capable of siring. Only human beings are capable of fatherhood.

MARGARET HALSEY
The Folks at Home

I don't mind owning I wished for a daughter. I can't
help thinking she would have resembled me more and
would have been perhaps easier to understand. This is a
selfish feeling, I admit: but boy or girl, they are very
interesting and infinitely touching.

JOSEPH CONRAD
Letter to Mrs. E. L. Sanderson, *February 26,1899*

The night you were born, I ceased being my father's
boy and became my son's father. That night I began
a new life.

HENRY GREGOR FELSEN
Letters to a Teen-Age Son

A boy wants something very special from his father.
You hear it said that fathers want their sons to be
what they feel they cannot themselves be, but I tell
you it also works the other way.

SHERWOOD ANDERSON
Memoirs

I think I was the last person whom he saw and
recognized. When he whispered my name, I felt a stab
of the fitness of it. Surely it is a good thing for a father,
in his final moments of consciousness, to know that
his son is near him. The father-son relation is the basic
link of continuity in life, carrying the male principle
and the tradition of responsibility from one
generation to the next.

MAX LERNER
The Unfinished Country

6. Women, Mothers

The very essence of motherly love is to care for
the child's growth, and that means to want the child's
separation from herself.

ERICH FROMM
The Art of Loving

Strangely enough, it is the over-idealization of the
maternal instinct which accounts for the thousands of
neglected children among us.

RUTH HERSCHBERGER
Adam's Rib

With grease and with grime, from corner to center,
Forever at war and forever alert.
No rest for a day lest the enemy enter;
I spend my whole life in struggle with dirt.

IRISH SONG
"The Housewife's Lament"

Mother for me made excuses
When I was a little tad;
Found some reason for my conduct
When it had been very bad.

EDGAR A. GUEST
"Mother's Excuses"

When I was single, I went dress'd so fine,
Now I am married, Lord, go ragged all the time.

Lord, I wish I was a single girl again.
Lord, I wish I was a single girl again.

AMERICAN FOLK SONG
"Single Girl"

Home is the girl's prison and the woman's workhouse.

GEORGE BERNARD SHAW
Maxims for Revolutionists

Sir, a woman's preaching is like a dog's walking
on his hind legs. It is not done well; but you are
surprised to find it done at all.

SAMUEL JOHNSON
in Boswell's Life of Samuel Johnson,
July 31, 1763

Man has his will—but woman has her way.

OLIVER WENDELL HOLMES
The Autocrat of the Breakfast-Table

The passivity that is the essential characteristic of
the "feminine" woman is a trait that develops in her
from the earliest years. But it is wrong to assert a
biological datum is concerned; it is in fact a destiny
imposed upon her by teachers and society.

SIMONE DE BEAUVOIR
The Second Sex

... The world runs better when men and women keep
to their own spheres. I do not say women are better off,
but society in general is. ... To say to us arbitrarily
as some psychologists and propagandists do, that it is
our *duty* to be busy elsewhere than at home is pretentious

nonsense. Few jobs are worth disrupting family life
for unless the family profits by it rather than the
housewife herself.

PHYLLIS MCGINLEY
Sixpence in Her Shoe

Women, as well as men, can only find their identity
in work that uses their full capacities. A woman cannot
find her identity through others—her husband, her
children. She cannot find it in the dull routine of
housework.

BETTY FRIEDAN
The Feminine Mystique

Mom got herself out of the nursery and the kitchen.
She then got out of the house ... she also got herself
the vote, and, although politics never interested her
(unless she was exceptionally naive, a hairy foghorn,
or a size 40 scorpion) the damage she forthwith did to
society was so enormous and so rapid that the best
men lost track of things.

PHILIP WYLIE
Generation of Vipers

The feminine mystique has succeeded in burying
millions of American women alive. There is no way for
these women to break out of their comfortable
concentration camps except by finally putting forth an
effort—that human effort which reaches beyond biology,
beyond the narrow walls of the home, to help shape
the future. Only by such a personal commitment to the
future can American women break out of the housewife
trap and truly find fulfillment as wives and mothers
by fulfilling their own unique possibilities as separate
human beings.

BETTY FRIEDAN
The Feminine Mystique

If what I did prove well, it won't advance;
They'll say it's stolen, or else it was by chance.

ANNE BRADSTREET

A woman cannot be herself in modern society, with
laws made by men and with prosecutors and judges
who assess female conduct from a male standpoint.

HENRIK IBSEN

Who can find a virtuous woman? For her price is far
above rubies. The heart of her husband doth safely
trust in her, so that he shall have no need of spoil. She
will do him good and not evil all the days of her life.

PROVERBS 31:10–12

Man's best possession is a sympathetic wife.

EURIPIDES

The only way to understand a woman is to love her—
and then it isn't necessary to understand her.

SYDNEY HARRIS
Strictly Personal

Women are called womanly only when they regard
themselves as existing solely for the use of men.

GEORGE BERNARD SHAW
Preface, Getting Married

Women have simple tastes. They can get pleasure out
of the conversation of children in arms and men in love.

H. L. MENCKEN
A Mencken Chrestomathy

Woman [is] the female of the human species, and not a different kind of animal.

GEORGE BERNARD SHAW
Preface, Saint Joan

A man is in general better pleased when he has a good dinner upon his table, than when his wife talks Greek.

SAMUEL JOHNSON
Miscellanies

Mother is the name for God in the lips and hearts of children.

WILLIAM MAKEPEACE THACKERAY
Vanity Fair

Woman's virtue is man's greatest invention.

CORNELIA OTIS SKINNER
Paris '90

All the pursuits of men are the pursuits of women also, but in all of them a woman is inferior to a man.

PLATO
The Republic

Frailty, thy name is woman!

WILLIAM SHAKESPEARE
Hamlet, *I:ii*

Be good, sweet maid, and let who can be clever.

CHARLES KINGSLEY
A Farewell

The hand that rocks the cradle
Is the hand that rules the world.

WILLIAM ROSS WALLACE
John o' London's Treasure Trove

Sleep my child, and peace attend thee
All through the night;
Guardian angels God will send thee,
All through the night.
Soft the drowsy hours are creeping,
Hill and vale in slumber sleeping,
I my loving vigil keeping,
All through the night.

> SIR HAROLD BOULTON
> *"All Through the Night"*

A good many men still like to think of their wives as they do of their religion, neglected but always there.

> FREYA STARK
> The Journey's Echo

Ascend a step to choose a friend, descend a step to choose a wife.

> THE TALMUD

She that weds well will wisely match her love,
Nor be below her husband nor above.

> OVID
> Heroides

To be loved—chosen by a good man is the best and sweetest thing which can happen to a woman.

> LOUISA MAY ALCOTT
> Little Women

Almost everybody allows himself or herself some entirely unjustifiable generalization on the subject of Woman. . . . For my part I distrust all generalizations about women, favorable and unfavorable, masculine and feminine, ancient and modern.

> BERTRAND RUSSELL
> *"An Outline of Intellectual Rubbish,"* Unpopular Essays

7. Childhood

It all lies in the unchanging realm of the past—this
land of my childhood. Its charm, its strange dominion
cannot return save in the poet's reminiscent dream.
No money, no railway train can take us back to it.
It did not in truth exist—it was a magical world,
born of the vibrant union of youth and firelight, of
music and the voice of moaning winds.

HAMLIN GARLAND
A Son of the Middle Border

... Children ... are the last candid audience left.
They don't care what critics say and they will let you
know immediately what delights and what bores them.

GIAN-CARLO MENOTTI
New York State Theater Magazine, *April 1971*

Your children are not your children.
They are the sons and daughters of Life's longing for itself
They come through you but not from you,
And though they are with you yet they belong not to you.
You may give them your love but not your thoughts,
For they have their own thoughts.
You may house their bodies but not their souls,
For their souls dwell in the house of tomorrow, which you
    cannot visit, not even in your dreams.
You may strive to be like them, but seek not to make
    them like you. ...

KAHLIL GIBRAN
The Prophet

The best brought-up children are those who have seen their parents as they are. Hypocrisy is not the parent's first duty.

GEORGE BERNARD SHAW
Maxims for Revolutionists

There is in every child at every stage a new miracle of vigorous unfolding, which constitutes a new hope and new responsibility for all. Such is the sense and pervading quality of initiative. The criteria for all these senses and qualities are the same: a crisis, more or less beset with fumbling and fear, is resolved, in that the child suddenly seems to "grow together" both in his person and his body.

ERIK ERIKSON
Childhood and Society

In an Indian home, if a child's face is dirty or his diaper is wet, he is picked up by anyone. The mother or father or whoever comes into the house. . . . And children are fed whenever they are hungry. They are never allowed to be in want.

WILFRED PELLETIER
This Book Is About Schools

When I think of your newborn children, of how you torture them in order to make them into "normal" human beings after your image. . . .

WILHELM REICH

Speak roughly to your little boy,
And beat him when he sneezes:
He only does it to annoy,
Because he knows it teases.

LEWIS CARROLL
Alice in Wonderland

Train up a child in the way he should go: and when
he is old, he will not depart from it.

PROVERBS 22:6

The amount of destructiveness in a child is
proportionate to the amount to which the expansiveness
of his life has been curtailed. Destructiveness is the
outcome of the unlived life.

ERICH FROMM

Children have two visions, the inner and the outer.
Of the two the inner vision is brighter.

SYLVIA ASHTON-WARNER
Teacher

How sharper than a serpent's tooth it is
To have a thankless child!

WILLIAM SHAKESPEARE
King Lear, I:iv

A child tells in the street what its father and mother
say at home.

THE TALMUD

He that spareth his rod hateth his son: but he that
loveth him chasteneth him betimes.

PROVERBS 13:24

Little children are still the symbol of the eternal
marriage between love and duty.

GEORGE ELIOT
Proem to Romola

Suffer the little children to come unto me, and forbid
them not: for of such is the kingdom of God.

MARK 10:14

A boy's will is the wind's will,
And the thoughts of youth are long, long thoughts.
HENRY WADSWORTH LONGFELLOW
"My Lost Youth"

Childhood is the form that upholds each child's life forever. If a man or a society taints a child's childhood, brutalizes it, strikes it down, and corrupts it with fear and bad dreams, then he maims that child forever, and the judgment on that man and that society will be terrible and eternal.
NED O'GORMAN
The Storefront

The hearts of small children are delicate organs. A cruel beginning in this world can twist them into curious shapes. The heart of a child can shrink so that forever afterward it is hard and pitted as the seed of a peach. Or again, the heart of such a child may fester and swell until it is a misery to carry within the body, easily chafed and hurt by the most ordinary things.
CARSON MC CULLERS

If you strike a child, take care that you strike it in anger, even at the risk of maiming it for life. A blow in cold blood neither can nor should be forgiven.
GEORGE BERNARD SHAW
Maxims for Revolutionists

Children are educated by what the grown-up is and not by his talk.
CARL G. JUNG
Psychological Reflections

He who sentimentally sings of blessed childhood is thinking of the return to nature and innocence and the

origin of things, and has quite forgotten that these
blessed children are beset with conflict and complexities
and capable of all suffering.

HERMANN HESSE

The average American child of the upper middle
class . . . is brought up in an atmosphere of Santa Claus;
and when he learns that Santa Claus is a myth,
he cries bitterly . . . and spends much of his later life
in the search for some emotional substitute.

NORBERT WIENER

Children are all foreigners. We treat them as such.

RALPH WALDO EMERSON

Mothers for miles around worried about Zuckerman's
swing. They feared some child would fall off. But no
child ever did. Children almost always hang onto things
tighter than their parents think they will.

E. B. WHITE
Charlotte's Web

"Listen, listen, the wind's talking," said John . . .
"Do you really mean we won't be able to hear *that*
when we're older, Mary Poppins?"
"You'll hear all right," said Mary Poppins, "but you
won't understand." At that Barbara began to weep gently.
There were tears in John's eyes, too. "Well, it can't be
helped. It's how things happen," said Mary Poppins
sensibly.

P. L. TRAVERS
Mary Poppins

40

8. Families

In peasant communities where things didn't change
and where people died in the beds they were born in,
grandparents taught the young what the end of life was
going to be. So you looked at your mother, if you were
a girl, and learned what it was like to be a bride,
a young mother. Then you looked at your grandmother
and you knew what it was like to be old. Children
learned what it was to age and die while they were
very small. They were prepared for the end of life
at the beginning.

MARGARET MEAD
The New York Times, *June 21, 1971*

All happy families resemble one another, each
unhappy family is unhappy in its own way.

LEO TOLSTOY
Anna Karenina

Therefore shall a man leave his father, and his mother,
and shall cleave unto his wife; and they shall be one flesh.

GENESIS 2:24

The original meaning of the word "family" (familia) . . .
is the total number of slaves belonging to one man.
The term was invented by the Romans to denote a new
social organism, whose head ruled over wife and

41

children and a number of slaves, and was invested
under Roman paternal power with rights of life and
death over them all.

FRIEDRICH ENGELS
The Origin of the Family,
Private Property and the State

"Oh dear," thought Meg, "married life is very trying,
and does need infinite patience, as well as love,
as mother says."

LOUISA MAY ALCOTT
Little Women

The parent who did not depend on love to influence
and mold the character of the child rather than force
would be regarded not as a real parent but a brute.
Force is worse than useless in developing the conduct
of the child.

CLARENCE DARROW
Resist Not Evil

Parental trust is extremely important in the guidance
of adolescent children as they get further and further
away from the direct supervision of their parents and
teachers. I don't mean that trust without clear guidance
is enough, but guidance without trust is worthless.

BENJAMIN SPOCK
Good Housekeeping, *May 1971*

"But, bless you, I'm her mother—
I can't talk to her, and, Lord, if I could!"

ROBERT FROST
"The Housekeeper"

All of us, I think, and not only the professional camp
followers of youth's army, have spent too much time

flattering our children. As teachers, we abdicate the role of teacher. As parents, we abdicate the role of parent. We wish to be colleagues and brothers and sisters, forgetting that the difference in age makes us look awkward. In the meantime we are tolerated, at best, by the young and, at worst, used.

SPENCER BROWN
"We Can't Appease the Younger Generation,"
The New York Times Magazine, *November 27, 1966*

Parents who are faced with the development of a number of children must constantly live up to a challenge. They must develop with them. We distort the situation if we abstract it in such a way that we consider the parent as having such and such a personality when the child is born and then, remaining stoic, impinging upon a poor little thing. For this weak and changing little being moves the whole family along. Babies control and bring up their families as much as they are controlled by them; in fact, we may say that the family brings up a baby by being brought up by him.

ERIK H. ERIKSON
Childhood and Society

And it seems possible to further paraphrase the relation of adult integrity and infantile trust that healthy children will not fear life if their elders have integrity enough not to fear death.

ERIK H. ERIKSON
Childhood and Society

The matter between husband and wife stands much the same as it does between two cocks in the same yard. The conqueror once is generally the conqueror for ever after. The prestige of victory is everything.

ANTHONY TROLLOPE
Barchester Towers

Intimates *trust* each other. They are not afraid that their partners will exploit their weaknesses. They take turns at giving and taking but are not concerned with contract-like reciprocity. They tactfully respect each other's belt lines and temper their honesty with infinite tact so that a partner will not be cruelly hurt.

GEORGE R. BACH and PETER WYDEN
The Intimate Enemy

A husband and wife ought to continue so long united as they love each other: any law which should bind them to cohabitation for one moment after the decay of their affection would be a most intolerable tyranny, and the most unworthy of toleration.

PERCY BYSSHE SHELLEY
Notes, "Queen Mab"

Married couples who love each other tell each other a thousand things without talking.

CHINESE PROVERB

Oh, what a tangled web do parents weave
When they think that their children are naive.

OGDEN NASH
"What Makes the Sky Blue?"

I tell you there's a wall ten feet thick and ten miles high between parent and child.

GEORGE BERNARD SHAW
Misalliance

The joys of parents are secret, and so are their griefs and fears.

FRANCIS BACON
"Of Parents and Children"

Wife and children are a kind of discipline of humanity.

FRANCIS BACON
"Of Marriage and Single Life"

Since having children does mean giving up so much, good parents naturally do, and should, expect something from their children in return: not spoken thanks for being born or being cared for—that's too much—but considerateness, affectionateness, and willingness to accept the parents' standards and ideals. The parents want these qualities in their children not only selfishly, for themselves, but because they want their children to grow up to live cooperatively and happily with others.

BENJAMIN SPOCK
Baby and Child Care

Children begin by loving their parents. After a time they judge them. Rarely, if ever, do they forgive them.

OSCAR WILDE
A Woman of No Importance

Home is the place where, when you have to go there, they have to take you in.

ROBERT FROST
"The Death of the Hired Man"

Taking care of their children, seeing them grow and develop into fine people, gives most parents—despite the hard work—their greatest satisfaction in life. This is creation. This is our visible immortality. Pride in other worldly accomplishments is usually weak in comparison.

BENJAMIN SPOCK
Baby and Child Care

I think most parents would agree that bringing up children in the present-day United States is both a

45

tentative and a taxing job. Indeed, the enormous American literature on child care is mute evidence that most American parents do not function parentally with easy and joyous self-confidence.

MARGARET HALSEY
The Folks at Home

Grown-ups love figures. When you tell them you have made a new friend, they never ask you any questions about essential matters. They never say to you, "What does his voice sound like? What games does he love best? Does he collect butterflies?" Instead, they demand: "How old is he? How many brothers has he? How much does he weigh? How much money does his father make?" Only from these figures do they think they have learned anything about him.

ANTOINE DE SAINT-EXUPÉRY
The Little Prince

A parent is his child's advocate. Like an attorney, he operates within the law. He does not condone misbehavior, or sanction misconduct. A lawyer does not encourage crime. He does not compliment a safe-cracker on his skill or a con man on his cunning. However, regardless of the offense he defends the accused. In the most difficult situations he tries to see the extenuating circumstances and to provide aid and hope.

HAIM G. GINOTT
Between Parent and Teen-ager

Families are the most beautiful things in all the world.

LOUISA MAY ALCOTT
Little Women

46

9. Old Age

Age is not a particularly interesting subject. Anyone can get old. All you have to do is live long enough.

GROUCHO MARX
Groucho and Me

The prosperity of a country is in accordance with its treatment of the aged.

HASIDIC SAYING

A man's heart is a grave long before he is buried. Youth dies, and beauty, and hope, and desire. A grave is buried within a grave when a man is buried.

ERIC HOFFER
The New York Times Magazine, *April 25, 1971*

The end comes when we no longer talk with ourselves. It is the end of genuine thinking and the beginning of the final loneliness.

The remarkable thing is that the cessation of the inner dialogue marks also the end of our concern with the world around us. It is as if we noted the world and think about it only when we have to report it to ourselves.

ERIC HOFFER
The New York Times Magazine, *April 25, 1971*

... When you get old, you can't talk to people because people snap at you. When you get so old, people talk to you that way. That's why you become deaf, so you won't be able to hear people talking to you that way. And that's why you go and hide under the covers in the big soft bed, so you won't feel the house shaking from people talking to you that way. That's why old people die, eventually. People talk to them that way.

EDWARD ALBEE
The American Dream

People don't say good-by to old people because they think they'll frighten them. Lordy! If they only knew how awful "hello" and "my, you're looking chipper" sounded, they wouldn't say those things either. The truth is, there isn't much you *can* say to old people that doesn't sound just terrible.

EDWARD ALBEE
The American Dream

To be seventy years young is sometimes far more hopeful than to be forty years old.

OLIVER WENDELL HOLMES

None are so old as those who have outlived enthusiasm.

HENRY DAVID THOREAU

With the ancient is wisdom; and in length of years understanding.

JOB 12:12

Every man who has lived his life to the full, should, by the time his senior years are reached, have established a reserve inventory of unfinished thinking.

CLARENCE B. RANDALL
Sixty-five Plus

48

"It's you," she said. "I can't get up. Forgive me
Not answering your knock. I can no more
Let people in than I can keep them out.
I'm getting too old for my size, I tell them.
My fingers are about all I've the use of
So's to take any comfort."

ROBERT FROST
"The Housekeeper"

Do not go gentle into that good night,
Old age should burn and rave at close of day;
Rage, rage against the dying of the light.

DYLAN THOMAS
"Do Not Go Gentle into that Good Night"

We can be dead certain that when our grandchildren
reach our age, they will not be living as we live today.

MARGARET MEAD
The New York Times, *June 12, 1971*

Even at my age of 85, I continue to learn every day.
I wish that while still possessing the knowledge and
wisdom acquired during these many years (which seem
so few to me now), I might be a young physician again,
hoping to enjoy life even more than I have enjoyed
my present life now drawing to a close.

PAUL DUDLEY WHITE
The New York Times, *October 10, 1971*

Youth, large, lusty, loving—youth full of grace, force,
    fascination,
Do you know that Old Age may come after you with
    equal grace, force, fascination?

WALT WHITMAN
"Youth, Day, Old Age and Night," Leaves of Grass

O the old manhood of me, my noblest joy of all!
My children and grand-children, my white hair and
  beard,
My largeness, calmness, majesty, out of the long stretch
  of my life.

WALT WHITMAN
"A Song of Joys," Leaves of Grass

Old age has a great sense of calm and freedom.
When the passions have relaxed their hold you have
escaped, not from one master, but from many.

PLATO
The Republic

Every man over forty is a scoundrel.

GEORGE BERNARD SHAW
Maxims for Revolutionists

The heart never grows better by age; I fear rather
worse; always harder. A young liar will be an old
one; and a young knave will only be a greater knave
as he grows older.

LORD CHESTERFIELD
Letters, May 17, 1750

The heads of strong old age are beautiful
Beyond all grace of youth.

ROBINSON JEFFERS
"Promise of Peace"

As a man advances in life he gets what is better
than admiration—judgment to estimate things at their
own value.

SAMUEL JOHNSON

But alas! the world grew younger as I grew older: its
vision cleared as mine dimmed: it began to read with
the naked eye the writing on the wall which now began
to remind me that the age of spectacles was at hand.
My opportunities were still there; nay, they multiplied
tenfold; but the strength and youth to cope with them
began to fail, and to need eking out with the shifty
cunning of experience.

GEORGE BERNARD SHAW
Preface, Plays Pleasant and Unpleasant

Not to be able to grow old is just as ridiculous as
to be unable to outgrow childhood.

CARL G. JUNG
Psychological Reflections

For the unlearned, old age is winter; for the learned,
it is the season of the harvest.

HASIDIC SAYING

I have had several applications, within a few years
past, from different persons, to furnish them with
materials for writing my life, and have uniformly
declined it on the ground of the decay of my memory,
the decline of the powers of body and mind, the
heaviness of age, and the crippled state of both my
hands, which renders writing the most painful labor I
can undertake.

THOMAS JEFFERSON
Letter to Robert Walsh, *April 5, 1823*

At seventy-five I have learned a little about the
structure of nature—of animals, plants and trees, birds,
fishes and insects. In consequence when I am eighty
I shall have made a little more progress. At ninety
I shall penetrate the mystery of things. At a hundred I

51

shall certainly have reached a marvelous stage, and
when I am a hundred and ten, everything I do—be it
a line or a dot—will be alive. I beg those who live
as long as I to see if I do not keep my word.
Written at the age of seventy-five by me, once Hokusai,
today The Old Man Mad about Drawing.

HOKUSAI

IV

"The Alternative to Despair"

10. Courage

Now the alternative to despair is *courage*. And human life can be viewed as a continuous struggle between these two options. Courage is the capacity to *affirm* one's life in spite of the elements which threaten it. The fact that courage usually predominates over despair in itself tells us something important about life. It tells us that the forces that affirm life are stronger than those that negate it.

> PAUL E. PFUETZE
> *"Sleeping Through a Revolution,"*
> Vassar Alumnae Quarterly, *Spring 1971*

You have to accept whatever comes and the only important thing is that you meet it with courage and with the best that you have to give.

> ELEANOR ROOSEVELT
> *in* Eleanor: The Years Alone
> *by Joseph P. Lash*

Have hope, brother,
Despair is for the defeated.

> OSWALD JOSEPH MTSHALI
> Sounds of a Cowhide Drum,
> The New York Times, *June 20, 1971*

The first and great commandment is, Don't let them scare you.

> ELMER DAVIS
> But We Were Born Free

Courage is the thing. All goes if courage goes.

JAMES M. BARRIE

A hero is no braver than an ordinary man, but he is brave five minutes longer.

RALPH WALDO EMERSON

A great part of courage is the courage of having done the thing before.

RALPH WALDO EMERSON

It is not difficult to be unconventional in the eyes of the world when your unconventionality is but the convention of your set.

W. SOMERSET MAUGHAM
The Moon and Sixpence

Fortune favors the brave.

TERENCE
Phormio

They tell us, sir, that we are weak—unable to cope with so formidable an adversary. But when shall we be stronger? Will it be the next week or the next year? Will it be when we are totally disarmed, and when a British guard shall be stationed in every house? Shall we gather strength by irresolution and inaction? . . . Sir, we are not weak, if we make a proper use of those forces which the God of nature hath placed in our power. Three millions of people armed in the holy cause of liberty, and in such a country as that which we possess, are invincible by any force which our enemy can send against us.

PATRICK HENRY
Address to the Virginia Convention, March 1775

The strongest man in the world is he who stands most alone.

HENRIK IBSEN
An Enemy of the People

That cause is strong which has not a multitude, but one strong man behind it.

JAMES RUSSELL LOWELL
Address, December 22, 1885

Desperate courage makes One a majority.

ANDREW JACKSON
in Life of Andrew Jackson, *by James Parton*

Before the echo had subsided, before the noise had completely registered on my consciousness, Agent Youngblood spun around, shoved me on the shoulder to push me down, and shouted to all of us, "Get down!" Almost in the same movement, he vaulted over the seat, pushed me to the floor, and sat on my right shoulder to keep me down and to protect me. "Get down!" he shouted again to all of us. Agent (Rufus) Youngblood's quick reaction was as brave an act as I have ever seen anyone perform. When a man, without a moment's thought or hesitation, places himself between you and a possible assassin's bullet, you know you have seen courage.

LYNDON B. JOHNSON
The Vantage Point

"What makes you a coward?" asked Dorothy, looking at the great beast in wonder, for he was as big as a small horse.

"It's a mystery," replied the Lion. "I suppose I was born that way. All the other animals in the forest naturally expect me to be brave, for the Lion is every-

where thought to be the King of Beasts. I learned that
if I roared very loudly every living thing was frightened
and got out of my way. Whenever I've met a man
I've been awfully scared; but I just roared at him and
he has always run away as fast as he could go. If
the elephants and the tigers and the bears had ever
tried to fight me, I should have run myself—I'm such
a coward; but just as soon as they hear me roar they
all try to get away from me, and of course I let them go."

L. FRANK BAUM
The Wizard of Oz

You have been told that, even like a chain, you are
as weak as your weakest link.

This is but half the truth. You are also as strong as
your strongest link.

To measure you by your smallest deed is to reckon
the power of the ocean by the frailty of its foam.

KAHLIL GIBRAN
The Prophet

"It is hard to be brave," said Piglet, sniffing slightly,
"when you're only a Very Small Animal."

A. A. MILNE
Winnie-The-Pooh

11. Joy and Happiness

No man is happy who does not think himself so.

PUBLILIUS SYRUS
Maxims

If happiness has not her seat
And center in the breast,
We may be wise or rich or great,
But never can be blest.

ROBERT BURNS
"Epistle to Davie"

Man is the artificer of his own happiness.

HENRY DAVID THOREAU
Journal, *January 21, 1838*

A merry heart maketh a cheerful countenance.

PROVERBS 15:13

Happiness is like coke—something you get as a
by-product in the process of making something else.

ALDOUS HUXLEY

The best way to cheer yourself is to try to cheer
somebody else up.

MARK TWAIN

Now to the banquet we press;
Now for the eggs and the ham;
Now for the mustard and cress,
Now for the strawberry jam!

WILLIAM S. GILBERT
The Sorcerer

We have no more right to consume happiness without
producing it than to consume wealth without
producing it.

GEORGE BERNARD SHAW
Candida

A happy life must be to a great extent a quiet life,
for it is only in an atmosphere of quiet that true joy
can live.

BERTRAND RUSSELL
The Conquest of Happiness

If the word happiness means anything, it means an
inner feeling of well-being, a sense of balance, a feeling
of being contented with life. These can exist only when
one feels free.

A. S. NEILL
Summerhill: A Radical Approach to Child Rearing

Weeping may endure for a night, but joy cometh
in the morning.

PSALMS 30:5

And I feel just as happy as a big sun-flow'r,
That nods and bends in the breezes;
And my heart's as light as the wind that blows
The leaves from off the trees-es.

TRADITIONAL AMERICAN SONG
"The Big Sunflower"

O happiness! our being's end and aim!
Good, pleasure, ease, content! whate'er thy name:
That something still which prompts the eternal sigh,
For which we bear to live, or dare to die.

ALEXANDER POPE
Essay on Man

We are never so happy, nor so unhappy, as we
suppose ourselves to be.

FRANÇOIS LA ROCHEFOUCAULD
Maxims

59

There comes
For ever something between us and what
We deem our happiness.

LORD BYRON
Sardanapalus

All who joy would win
Must share it,—Happiness was born a twin.

LORD BYRON
Don Juan

Teach me half the gladness
    That thy brain must know,
Such harmonious madness
From my lips would flow,
The world would listen then, as I am
    listening now.

PERCY BYSSHE SHELLEY
"To A Skylark"

If all the griefs I am to have
Would only come today,
I am so happy I believe
They'd laugh and run away.

EMILY DICKINSON

12. Self-Acceptance

A person cannot be fully aware of the world unless
he has some capacity to understand the manner in which
he perceives that world. Self-understanding also implies
being at ease with one's past. The healthy man cannot

live wholly in the present nor can he base his existence
on future rewards.

SEYMOUR L. HALLECK
"Why They'd Rather Do Their Own Thing"
in Now and Tomorrow

Divine am I inside and out, and I make holy whatever I
touch or am touch'd from,
The scent of these arm-pits aroma finer than prayer ...

WALT WHITMAN
"Song of Myself," Leaves of Grass

People will do anything, no matter how absurd, in
order to avoid facing their own soul.

CARL G. JUNG
Psychological Reflections

I am a free man, an American, a United States
Senator and a Democrat in that order. I am also a
liberal, a conservative, a Texan, a taxpayer, a rancher,
a businessman, a consumer, a parent, a voter, and not as
young as I used to be nor as old as I expect to be—
and I am all these things in no fixed order.

LYNDON B. JOHNSON
on seeking Democratic Presidential nomination in 1960,
Christian Science Monitor, *November 27, 1963*

I don't have to be what you want me to be.

MUHAMMAD ALI

A man's hatred is always concentrated upon that
which makes him conscious of his bad qualities.

CARL G. JUNG
Psychological Reflections

Know thyself. A maxim as pernicious as it is ugly.
Whoever studies himself arrests his own development.

A caterpillar that set out really to "know itself" would never become a butterflv.

ANDRÉ GIDE
Journal

One's philosophy is not best expressed in words; it is expressed in the choices one makes. . . . In the long run, we shape our lives and we shape ourselves. The process never ends until we die. And the choices we make are ultimately our responsibility.

ELEANOR ROOSEVELT

No one can make you feel inferior without your consent.

ELEANOR ROOSEVELT

What and how much had I lost by trying to do only what was expected of me instead of what I myself had wished to do? What a waste, what a senseless waste.

RALPH ELLISON
The Invisible Man

I have to live with myself, and so
I want to be fit for myself to know;
I want to be able as days go by,
Always to look myself straight in the eye.
I don't want to stand with the setting sun
And hate myself for the things I've done.

EDGAR A. GUEST
"Myself"

To know what you prefer, instead of humbly saying Amen to what the world tells you you ought to prefer, is to have kept your soul alive.

ROBERT LOUIS STEVENSON
"The Royal Sport Nautique"

"Maggie, we were both born of many errors; a human
being has to forgive himself! Neither of us is innocent.
What more do you want?"

ARTHUR MILLER
After the Fall

In the time of your life—live!

WILLIAM SAROYAN
The Time of Your Life

The duty to be alive is the same as the duty to become
oneself, to develop into the individual one potentially is.

ERICH FROMM
Man for Himself

. . . At nineteen I was a stranger to myself. At forty
I asked: Who am I? At fifty I concluded I would never
know.

EDWARD DAHLBERG
The New York Times Book Review, *January 31, 1971*

What we start with is a conviction to fulfill our being.
Horses, trees fulfill themselves. Why shouldn't people?

LOUISE NEVELSON
The New York Times Magazine, *January 24, 1971*

Self-love, my liege, is not so vile a sin
As self-neglecting.

WILLIAM SHAKESPEARE
Henry V, *II:iv*

Even the knowledge of my own fallibility cannot keep
me from making mistakes; only when I fall do I get up
again . . .

VINCENT VAN GOGH
Letters to An Artist

My motto for the home, in education as in life, is this:
For heaven's sake, let people live their own lives. It is
an attitude that fits any situation.

A. S. NEILL
Summerhill: A Radical Approach to Child Rearing

The kinds of people who can go on to greater emotional
maturity are those who really like themselves, even if
the world seems to turn against them. Their self-worth
does not rest on events, but on their opinions of
themselves. Their inner security lies in the confidence
that they will be able to contend with bad breaks; if
they can't change the situation, they will nevertheless
somehow endure. They take reverses as part of the
normal pattern of living.

THEODORE IRWIN
How to Cope with Crises

I do my thing, and you do your thing.
I am not in this world to live up to
        your expectations
And you are not in this world to live
        up to mine.
You are you and I am I,
And if by chance we find each other,
        it's beautiful.
If not, it can't be helped.

FREDERICK S. PERLS

I celebrate myself, and sing myself,
And what I assume you shall assume,
For every atom belonging to me as good belongs to you.
I loafe and invite my soul,
I lean and loafe at my ease observing a spear of
        summer grass.

WALT WHITMAN
"Song of Myself," Leaves of Grass

64

13. Fantasy and Imagination

"Then how could you have been there? It couldn't
have been our Fairyland!"
Mary Poppins gave a superior sniff.
"Don't you know," she said pityingly, "that everybody's got a Fairyland of their own?"

P. L. TRAVERS
Mary Poppins

Imagination is more important than knowledge.

ALBERT EINSTEIN
"On Science"

Build of your imaginings a bower in the wilderness ere
you build a house within the city walls.

KAHLIL GIBRAN
The Prophet

A man may die, nations may rise and fall, but an
idea lives on. Ideas have endurance without death.

JOHN F. KENNEDY
Address, Greenville, North Carolina, February 8, 1963

Ideas won't keep. Something must be done about
them.

ALFRED NORTH WHITEHEAD
Dialogues

To make a prairie it takes a clover and one bee,
One clover, and a bee,

And revery.
The revery alone will do,
If bees are few.

EMILY DICKINSON

A definition is the enclosing a wilderness of idea
within a wall of words.

SAMUEL BUTLER
Notebooks

A new idea is delicate. It can be killed by a sneer or
a yawn; it can be stabbed to death by a quip and
worried to death by a frown on the right man's brow.

CHARLES BROWER
Advertising Age, *August 10, 1959*

Every new opinion, at its starting, is precisely in a
minority of one.

THOMAS CARLYLE
Heroes and Hero-Worship

One's thoughts fly so fast that one must shoot them;
it is no use trying to put salt on their tails.

SAMUEL BUTLER
Preface, Notebooks

A play should give you something to think about.
When I see a play and understand it the first time, then
I know it can't be much good.

T. S. ELIOT
New York Post, *September 22, 1963*

The truth of an idea is not a stagnant property
inherent in it. Truth *happens* to an idea. It *becomes*
true, is *made* true by events.

WILLIAM JAMES
"On Pragmatism"

O, who can hold a fire in his hand
By thinking on the frosty Caucasus?
Or cloy the hungry edge of appetite
By bare imagination of a feast?
Or wallow naked in December snow
By thinking on fantastic summer's heat?
Oh, no! the apprehension of the good
Gives but the greater feeling to the worse.

WILLIAM SHAKESPEARE
Richard II, I:3

When I could not sleep for cold
I had fire enough in my brain
And builded with roofs of gold
My beautiful castles in Spain.

JAMES RUSSELL LOWELL
"Aladdin"

We do not really mean, we do not really mean, that
what we are going to say is true.

TRADITIONAL ASHANTI FOLKTALE BEGINNING

This, my story which I have related, if it be sweet or
if it be not sweet, take some elsewhere and let some
come back to me.

TRADITIONAL ASHANTI FOLKTALE ENDING

We go to the beach
I look at the sea
My mother thinks I stare
My father thinks I want to go in the water.
But I have my own little world.

AMY LEVY
grade six,
"My Own Little World"
in Wishes, Lies and Dreams *by Kenneth Koch*

V

"Citizens of the World, Members of the Human Community"

14. My Country, My World

We have learned that we cannot live alone, in peace; that our own well-being is dependent on the well-being of other nations, far away. . . . We have learned to be citizens of the world, members of the human community.

FRANKLIN D. ROOSEVELT
Fourth Inaugural Address, January 20, 1945

My country is the world, and my religion is to do good.

THOMAS PAINE
The Rights of Man

And hath made of one blood all nations of men for to dwell on all the face of the earth.

ACTS 17:26

I am not an Athenian nor a Greek, but a citizen of the world.

SOCRATES

Our country is the world; our countrymen are all mankind.

WILLIAM LLOYD GARRISON
"Prospectus," The Liberator, *December 15, 1837*

Great problems usually come to the United Nations because governments have been unable to think of anything else to do about them.

U THANT
The New York Times, *September 21, 1971*

When we started the UN we were not trying to make a monument. We were building a workshop—a workshop for world peace. And we tried to make it the best damn workshop we could.

WALLACE HARRISON
Time, *September 22, 1952*

All men—whether they go by the name of Americans or Russians or Chinese or British or Malayans or Indians or Africans—have obligations to one another that transcend their obligations to their sovereign societies.

NORMAN COUSINS
In Place of Folly

A man's feet should be planted in his country, but his eyes should survey the world.

GEORGE SANTAYANA

Everybody likes to hear about a man laying down his life for his country, but nobody wants to hear about a country giving her shirt for her planet.

E. B. WHITE
World Government and Peace

When I say that peace must be planned on a world basis, I mean quite literally that it must embrace the earth. . . . It is inescapable that there can be no peace for any part of the world unless the foundations of peace are made secure throughout all parts of the world.

WENDELL WILKIE
One World

What we call foreign affairs is no longer foreign affairs. It's a local affair. Whatever happens in Indonesia is important to Indiana. Whatever happens in any corner of the world has some effect on the farmer in Dickinson County, Kansas, or on a worker in a factory.

DWIGHT D. EISENHOWER
Address, Foreign Service Institute, June 12, 1959

Patriotism is the last refuge of a scoundrel.

SAMUEL JOHNSON
in Boswell's Life of Samuel Johnson,
April 7, 1775

Patriotism is a kind of religion; it is the egg from which wars are hatched.

GUY DE MAUPASSANT
"My Uncle Sosthenes"

One of the great attractions of patriotism—it fulfills our worst wishes. In the person of our nation we are able, vicariously, to bully and cheat. Bully and cheat, what's more, with a feeling that we are profoundly virtuous.

ALDOUS HUXLEY
Eyeless in Gaza

Patriotism is your conviction that this country is superior to all other countries because you were born in it.

GEORGE BERNARD SHAW

Nationalism is an infantile disease. It is the measles of mankind.

ALBERT EINSTEIN

The selfishness of nations is proverbial. It was a
dictum of George Washington that nations were not to
be trusted beyond their own self interest.

REINHOLD NIEBUHR

The structure of world peace cannot be the work of
one man, or one party, or one nation. It cannot be an
American peace, or a British peace, or a Russian, or a
French or a Chinese peace. It cannot be a peace of
large nations—or of small nations. It must be a peace
which rests on the cooperative effort of the whole
world....

FRANKLIN D. ROOSEVELT
upon his return from the Yalta conference, 1945

Have we not all one Father? Hath not one God
created us?

MALACHI 11:10

15. History

We can think of history as a kind of layer cake in
which a number of different layers run side by side
through time, each with a dynamic of its own, and yet
each from time to time profoundly penetrating and
interacting with others.

KENNETH E. BOULDING
"Technology and the Changing Social Order"
in The Urban Industrial Frontier

All historians, even the most scientific, have bias, if in no other sense than the determination not to have any.
CARL BECKER
Everyman His Own Historian

———

There cannot be a new History, in the sense our younger malcontents are calling for it—that is, a History researched, written and taught in such a way as to aid directly in the eradication of social ills—because we can neither manufacture the needed data for "problem-solving" nor decontaminate the scholars who will deal with it. For those among the young, historians and otherwise, who are chiefly interested in changing the present, I can only say, speaking from my own experience, that they doom themselves to bitter disappointment if they seek their guides to action in a study of the past.
MARTIN DUBERMAN
The Uncompleted Past

———

Let us then admit that there are two histories: the actual series of events that once occurred; and the ideal series that we affirm and hold in memory. The first is absolute and unchanged—it was what it was whatever we do or say about it; the second is relative, always changing in response to the increase or refinement of knowledge. The two series correspond more or less, it is our aim to make the correspondence as exact as possible; but the actual series of events exists for us only in terms of the ideal series which we affirm and hold in memory.
CARL BECKER
Everyman His Own Historian

———

I care for the great deeds of the past chiefly as spurs to drive us onward in the present. I speak of the men of the past partly that they may be honored by our

praise of them, but more that they may serve as
examples for the future.

THEODORE ROOSEVELT
The New Nationalism

The follies of our own times are easier to bear when
they are seen against the background of past follies.

BERTRAND RUSSELL
"An Outline of Intellectual Rubbish," Unpopular Essays

Our American past always speaks to us with two
voices: the voice of the past, and the voice of the present.
We are always asking two quite different questions.
Historians reading the words of John Winthrop usually
ask, "What did they mean to him?" Citizens ask, "What
do they mean to us?" Historians are trained to seek the
original meaning; all of us want to know the present
meaning.

DANIEL J. BOORSTIN
An American Primer

The historian does collect evidence, usually in the
form of records of what happened, but he can never
prove that the records are infallible or that he has all the
pertinent evidence. Furthermore, he can never divest
himself of his own point of view. For these reasons the
historian's conclusions are always tentative, never
universally accepted, and are almost certain to be dis-
carded partially or totally by his successors.

WALTER PRESCOTT WEBB
An Honest Preface

What the historian does as he peers into the
kaleidoscopic past is this: he tries to see relationships
among the varied past activities of man. He searches
for connections, appraises forces and treats them as

causes operating to produce resultant effects. . . . The patterns can never be touched or tested by the senses; they can only be described as they appear to the informed and questing mind.

WALTER PRESCOTT WEBB
An Honest Preface

History may perhaps have an end; but our task is not to terminate history, but to create it.

ALBERT CAMUS

. . . The young today need to learn that there has been change. They need to know about their past before they can understand the present and plot the future.

MARGARET MEAD
The New York Times, *June 12, 1971*

Political history is far too criminal a subject to be a fit thing to teach children.

W. H. AUDEN
The New York Times, *December 16, 1970*

The illusion that times that were are better than those that are, has probably pervaded all ages.

HORACE GREELEY
The American Conflict

Human history becomes more and more a race between education and catastrophe.

H. G. WELLS
The Outline of History

No great man lives in vain. The history of the world is but the biography of great men.

THOMAS CARLYLE
Heroes and Hero-Worship

History has nothing to record save wars and revolutions: the peaceful years appear only as brief pauses or interludes, scattered here and there.

ARTHUR SCHOPENHAUER
Parerga and Paralipomena

History can be well written only in a free country.

VOLTAIRE
Letter to Frederick the Great, May 27, 1737

History is only a confused heap of facts.

LORD CHESTERFIELD
Letters, February 5, 1750

The principal office of history I take to be this: to prevent virtuous actions from being forgotten, and that evil words and deeds should fear an infamous reputation with posterity.

TACITUS
Annals

To be ignorant of what occurred before you is to remain always a child. For what is the worth of human life, unless it is woven into the life of our ancestors by the records of history.

CICERO

History is little more than the register of the crimes, follies, and misfortunes of mankind.

EDWARD GIBBON
Decline and Fall of the Roman Empire

History is on every occasion the record of that which one age finds worthy of note in another.

JAKOB BURCKHARDT

History is bunk.

History is full of surprises.

ARTHUR M. SCHLESINGER, JR.
in Playboy Interviews

History is a living horse laughing at a wooden-horse.
History is a wind blowing where it listeth.
History is no sure thing to bet on.
History is a box of tricks with a lost key.
History is a labyrinth of doors with sliding panels, a book
of ciphers with the code in a cave of the Saragossa sea.
History says, if it pleases, Excuse me, I beg your
pardon, it will never happen again if I can help it.

CARL SANDBURG
"Good Morning, America"

16. Civilization and Culture

In the beginning, God gave to every people a cup,
a cup of clay, and from this cup they drank their life.

OLD DIGGER INDIAN
quoted by Ruth Benedict in An Anthropologist At Work

It seems that the line of Culture is continuous, without
short cuts, unbroken from the unknown Beginning to
the unknown End.

JOSÉ CLEMENTE OROZCO

Men in all societies possess the biological equipment to remove their hats or shoes, but it is the birth within a particular culture that decides that a Jew will keep his hat and his shoes on in his place of worship, a Mohammedan will take off his shoes, and a Christian will keep his shoes on but remove his hat.

PETER FARB
Man's Rise to Civilization as Shown by
The Indians of North America

. . . The art of letters, though highly developed grammatically, is still in its infancy as a technical speech notation: for example, there are fifty ways of saying Yes, and five hundred of saying No, but only one way of writing them down.

GEORGE BERNARD SHAW
Preface, Plays Pleasant and Unpleasant, *1898*

We must accept all the implications of our human inheritance, one of the most important of which is the small scope of biologically transmitted behavior, and the enormous role of the cultural process of the transmission of tradition.

RUTH BENEDICT
Patterns of Culture

The habits of any culture fit the people who learn to use them like well-worn gloves. This fit goes very deep, for their ideas of right and wrong, their selection of human desires and passions, are part and parcel of their whole version of culture. They can react to another people's way of conducting life with a supreme lack of interest or at least of comprehension. Among civilized peoples, this often appears in their depreciation of "foreign ways"; it is easy to develop a blind spot where another people's cherished customs are concerned.

RUTH BENEDICT
"The Growth of Culture,"
in The New Treasury of Science

It is easier to shift from being a South Sea Islander to being a New Yorker—as I have seen Samoans do—than to shift from being a perfectly adjusted traditional South Sea Islander to a partly civilized, partly acculturated South Sea Islander, who has been given antiquated versions of our philosophy and politics, a few odds and ends of clothing and furniture, and bits and pieces of our economics.

MARGARET MEAD
New Lives for Old

You think that a wall as solid as the earth separates civilization from barbarism. I tell you the division is a thread, a sheet of glass. A touch here, a push there, and you bring back the reign of Saturn.

JOHN BUCHAN

The civilized man has built a coach, but has lost the use of his feet.

RALPH WALDO EMERSON
"Self-Reliance"

Civilization is a stream with banks. The stream is sometimes filled with blood from people killing, stealing, shouting and doing the things historians usually record, while on the banks, unnoticed people build homes, make love, raise children, sing songs, write poetry and even whittle statues. The story of civilization is the story of what happened on the banks. Historians are pessimists because they ignore the banks for the river.

WILL DURANT

The myths of society are what give a person the ability to handle anxiety, to face death, and to deal with guilt. Our society is sick because it has lost the language

by which it communicates with the meaningful crises
of life.

ROLLO MAY
The New York Times Magazine, *March 28, 1971*

The fundamental patterns of behavior laid down in
our early days as hunting apes still shine through all
our affairs, no matter how lofty they may be.

DESMOND MORRIS
The Naked Ape

While Darwinian Man, though well-behaved,
At best is only a monkey shaved!

WILLIAM S. GILBERT
Princess Ida

Behind the facade of modern city life there is the
same old naked ape. Only the names have been
changed: for "hunting" read "working," for "hunting
grounds" read "place of business," for "home base"
read "house," for "pair-bond" read "marriage," for
"mate" read "wife," and so on.

DESMOND MORRIS
The Naked Ape

Man became not merely one of the beasts that mated,
fought for its food, and died, but a human being, with
a name, a position, and a god. Each people makes
this fabric differently, selects some clues and ignores
others, emphasizes a different sector of the whole arc of
human potentialities.

MARGARET MEAD
Sex and Temperament

We didn't always live at home. We lived wherever
we happened to be at that particular time when it got

dark. If you were two or three miles away from home, then that is where you slept. People would feed you even if they didn't know who you were.

WILFRED PELLETIER
This Book Is About Schools

Government is a contrivance of human wisdom to provide for human wants. Men have a right that these wants should be provided for by this wisdom.

EDMUND BURKE
Reflections on the Revolution in France

Our culture has not been very successful. Our education, politics, and economics lead to war. Our medicines have not done away with disease. Our religion has not abolished usury and robbery. Our boasted humanitarianism still allows public opinion to approve of the barbaric sport of hunting. The advances of the age are advances in mechanism—in radio and television, in electronics, in jet planes. New world wars threaten, for the world's social conscience is still primitive.

A. S. NEILL
Summerhill: A Radical Approach to Child Rearing

The Frisbee satisfies many present-day demands. It is easily mass produced. It is space-minded and in fact looks something like a U.F.O. And in keeping with the pop culture of our times, the toy appears temptingly simple and simpleminded. In reality, however, it is bewilderingly complex and deceptive. It plays unpredictable tricks on its participants and even confounds its own natural element, the air. Like contemporary history and the beguiling events taking place in it, the Frisbee seems to be within our grasp one moment while slipping away from us the next.

ALBERT L. WEEKS
The New York Times, August 2, 1971

82

Members of the human race have a right to just one
great boast: that they have an endless capacity to
invent and learn. They can learn not merely as other
mammals do, from imitation and from individual
experience, but from experience passed down to a
present generation from thousands of forebears now
dead and gone.

RUTH BENEDICT
"The Growth of Culture,"
in The New Treasury of Science

The divisions into classes . . . are not artificial.
They are the natural outcome of a civilised society. . . .
There must always be a master and servants in all
civilised communities . . . for it is natural, and whatever
is natural is right.

JAMES M. BARRIE
The Admirable Crichton

From father to son, so it goes on.

ASHANTI PROVERB

17. War and Peace

War is an old, old plant on this earth, and a natural
history of it would have to tell us under what soil
conditions it grows, where it plays havoc, and how it is
eliminated. Control of war cannot be based on anything
less than such knowledge, and until our efforts are thus
grounded despair is premature.

RUTH BENEDICT
"The Natural History of War,"
An Anthropologist at Work

It is raining now and everybody is soaked to the skin, but the oldtimers tell me I'll get used to it. Maybe I will. I would like to make a wish that when this war is over, none of my friends or the new generation will ever have to go anywhere to fight.

GI IN VIETNAM
Letter to "Dear Abby,"
New York Post, *January 4, 1971*

There never was a good war or a bad peace.

BENJAMIN FRANKLIN
Letter, September 11, 1783

I am writing my own obituary. . . .
I loved the Army: it reared me, it nurtured me, and it gave me the most satisfying years of my life. Thanks to it I have lived an entire lifetime in 26 years. It is only fitting that I should die in its service. . . .
And yet I deny that I died FOR anything—not my country, not my Army, not my fellow man. I LIVED for these things, and the manner in which I chose to do it involved the very real chance that I would die in the execution of my duties. . . .
. . . The Army is my life, it is such a part of what I was that what happened is the logical outcome of the life I loved. I never knew what it is to be too old or too tired to do anything. I lived a full life in the Army, and it has exacted the price. It is only just.

MAJOR JOHN ALEXANDER HOTTELL
written for the West Point Alumni Quarterly, The Assembly, about one year before his death in a helicopter crash, July 7, 1970, reprinted in The New York Times, March 3, 1971

This is the way the world ends
Not with a bang but a whimper.

T. S. ELIOT
"The Hollow Men"

Now it seems to me that, from the point of view of
statecraft,—no war is justifiable which does not solve a
question. A war should be a final act.

JOSEPH CONRAD

Letter to E. L. Sanderson, *October 26, 1899*

―――――

War is simply a social invention. But once it was
invented, one group could use it to overcome or defend
itself against another organized group. Right through
history, war has paid. And as there was always the
possibility of being a victor, it was very difficult
to eliminate war.

MARGARET MEAD

A Way of Seeing

―――――

The central question emerging from this problem, of
course, is whether any nation, even in its own defense,
has the right to tear down half the rest of the world
and damage the prospects of all mankind.

NORMAN COUSINS

In Place of Folly

―――――

Man today is not safe in the presence of man. The
old cannibalism has given way to anonymous action in
which the killer and the killed do not know each other,
and in which, indeed, the very fact of mass death
has the effect of making the killing less reprehensible
than the death of a single man.

In short, man has evolved in every respect except his
ability to protect himself against human intelligence.

NORMAN COUSINS

In Place of Folly

―――――

They shall beat their swords into plowshares, and
their spears into pruning-hooks: nation shall not lift up
sword against nation, neither shall they learn war any
more.

ISAIAH 2:4

War has always been the chief promoter of governmental power. The control of government over the private citizen is always greater where there is war or imminent danger of war than where peace seems secure.

BERTRAND RUSSELL
"Ideas That Have Helped Mankind," Unpopular Essays

... Every time we make a nuclear weapon, we corrupt the morals of a host of innocent neutrons below the age of consent.

W. H. AUDEN
The New York Times, *February 2, 1971*

Sometime they'll give a war and nobody will come.

CARL SANDBURG
"The People, Yes"

Each peaceful gesture, each little thing, each humble effort at pacification, accomplished at any level, brings peace closer. The journey of a thousand leagues begins with a single step. We must never neglect any work of peace that is within our reach, however small. We have constantly to carry on, or re-begin, the work of building the institutions and practices of a nonviolent world, keeping always in mind, beyond the setbacks and disappointments, our own vision of a peaceful future for men.

ADLAI E. STEVENSON
Looking Outward

Peace is that state in which fear of any kind is unknown.

JOHN BUCHAN

All states affirm that they want peace, and at the same time arm themselves against one another.

LEO TOLSTOY

We know that enduring peace cannot be bought at
the cost of other people's freedom.

FRANKLIN D. ROOSEVELT

There is such a thing as a man being too proud to
fight. There is such a thing as a nation being so right
that it does not need to convince others by force that
it is right. . . .

WOODROW WILSON

I went ashore and saw the barbed wire, the machine
guns and a "woodpile" of dead Vietcong bodies, and it
hit me all at once. This was my first contact with the
land war, and at first it looked like something out of
the movies. Then I realized—I said "My God, what is
going on here—this is really a war."

JOHN FORBES KERRY
after leading a demonstration
of Vietnam Veterans Against the War,
The New York Times, April 23, 1971

When we add divisions can't the enemy add
divisions? If so, where does it all end?

LYNDON B. JOHNSON
conversation with General Westmoreland, April 27, 1967,
The Pentagon Papers

War is nothing more than the continuation of politics
by other means.

KARL VON CLAUSEWITZ
On War

Men grow tired of sleep, love, singing and dancing
sooner than of war.

HOMER
Iliad

"I Did Not Raise My Boy to Be A Soldier."

ALFRED BRYAN
Song title

Soldiers ought more to fear their general than their enemy.

MONTAIGNE
Essays

A soldier is an anachronism.

GEORGE BERNARD SHAW
The Devil's Disciple

"Peace upon earth!" was said. We sing it
And pay a million priests to bring it.
After two thousand years of mass
We've got as far as poison-gas.

THOMAS HARDY
"Christmas: 1924"

There is many a boy here today who looks on war as all glory, but, boys, it is all hell.

WILLIAM T. SHERMAN
Address, Columbus, Ohio, August 11, 1880

War is not healthy for children and other living things.

sign carried by a schoolgirl on
Moratorium Day, October 15, 1969,
The New York Times, *October 16, 1969*

The event corresponds less to expectations in war than in any other case whatever.

LIVY
History of Rome

To overcome in battle, and subdue
Nations, and bring home spoils with infinite
Man-slaughter, shall be held the highest pitch
Of human glory.

JOHN MILTON
Paradise Lost

If our air forces are never used, they have achieved
their finest goal.

NATHAN F. TWINING
International News Service, *March 31, 1956*

War is like a giant pack rat. It takes something from
you, and it leaves something behind in its stead. It
burned me out in some ways, so that now I feel like an
old man, but still sometimes act like a dumb kid. It
made me grow up too fast.

AUDIE MURPHY
New York Journal-American, *August 30, 1955*

The mere absence of war is not peace.

JOHN F. KENNEDY
State of the Union Message, January 24, 1963

In my dreams I hear again the crash of guns, the
rattle of musketry, the strange, mournful mutter of the
battlefield. But in the evening of my memory always I
come back to West Point. Always there echoes and
re-echoes: Duty, honor, country.

DOUGLAS MACARTHUR
Address at West Point, May 12, 1962

War can only be abolished through war, and in order
to get rid of the gun it is necessary to take up the gun.

MAO TSE-TUNG

In war there is no substitute for victory.

DOUGLAS MACARTHUR
Address before Joint Meeting of Congress, April 19, 1951

i have noticed
that when
chickens quit
quarrelling over their
food they often
find that there is
enough for all of them
i wonder if
it might not
be the same way
with the
human race

DON MARQUIS
"random thoughts by archy,"
Archys Life of Mehitabel

VI

"This Land Is Your Land"

18. America: Rights and Wrongs

This land is your land, this land is my land,
From California to the New York Island,
From the redwood forest, to the gulf stream waters,
This land was made for you and me.

WOODY GUTHRIE
"This Land is Your Land"

America ranks with Greece and Rome as one of the
great distinct civilizations of history.

MAX LERNER
America As a Civilization

My countrymen have now become too base,
I give them up. I cannot speak with men
not my equals. I was an American,
where now to drag my days out and erase
this awful memory of the United States?

PAUL GOODMAN
"April 1962," The Lordly Hudson

I love America because nobody pays attention to my
accent. Only out of curiosity do people ask me "where
are you from?" They accept me for what I am. They
do not question my ancestry, my faith, my political
beliefs. I love this country because when I want to move
from one place to another I do not have to ask
permission. Because when I want to go abroad I just
buy a ticket and go . . .

I love America because America trusts me. When I go into a shop to buy a pair of shoes I am not asked to produce my Identity Card. I love it because my mail is not censored. My phone is not tapped. My conversation with friends is not reported to the secret police.

JANINA ATKINS
Polish-born student,
Thanksgiving Day statement,
The New York Times, *November 26, 1970*

We have no hope of solving our problems without harnessing the diversity, the energy and the creativity of all our people.

ROGER WILKINS
The New York Times, *December 22, 1970*

Perhaps our gravest fault as a nation is our exalted sense of American virtue. We see the United States as something unique in the world, a nation whose concerns soar above petty national ambitions, whose generosity and goodwill are unequalled. God, we assume, is invariably on our side thanks to a special convenant with the Almighty.

REINHOLD NIEBUHR
quoted in obituary, The New York Times, *June 2, 1971*

What do we want with this vast, worthless area? This region of savages and wild beasts, of deserts, of shifting sands and whirlwinds of dust, of cactus and prairie dogs? To what use could we ever hope to put these great deserts, or those endless mountain ranges, impenetrable and covered to their very base with eternal snow? What can we ever hope to do with the western coast, a coast of three thousand miles, rockbound, cheerless, uninviting, and not a harbor on it? What use have we for this country?

DANIEL WEBSTER
Address in the Senate, 1829,
opposing a bill to open a mail route
to the West Coast

I came from a rural region, where people have a
hard time. They don't have time for wittily observing the
things around them. They're not concerned about
anything more than existing from day to day.
They're not stupid. They're ignorant. Everything is
ugly around them—the architecture, the town, the
clothing they wear. Everything they see is ugly.

BARBARA LODEN
The New York Times, March 11, 1971

This will never be a civilized country until we
expend more money for books than we do for
chewing gum.

ELBERT HUBBARD
The Philistine

Ours is the only country deliberately founded on a
good idea.

JOHN GUNTHER
Inside U.S.A.

The whole drift of our law is toward the absolute
prohibition of all ideas that diverge in the slightest
from the accepted platitudes, and behind that drift of
law there is a far more potent force of growing custom,
and under that custom there is a natural philosophy
which erects conformity into the noblest of virtues and
the free functioning of personality into a capital crime
against society.

H. L. MENCKEN
The Vintage Mencken

The United States is the first authentic world power.
Since it is also the richest and most powerful country,
it cannot but inspire mixed feelings—envy and
resentment combined with admiration or fear.

RAYMOND ARON
in As Others See Us

94

Well, you know, a lot of Americans are unbalanced.
I don't care what you say. No, really. A lot of them are
quite normal, of course, but we've met many unbalanced
ones.

PAUL MC CARTNEY
in Playboy Interviews

When one reflects that half a dozen Presidents in this
century have been targets of assassination attempts,
the notion that we have been a great virtuous
country of law and order is hard to sustain.

ARTHUR M. SCHLESINGER, JR.
in Playboy Interviews

To the frontier the American intellect owes
its striking characteristics. That coarseness and
strength combined with acuteness and inquisitiveness;
that practical, inventive turn of mind, quick to find
expedients; that masterful grasp of material things,
lacking in the artistic but powerful to effect great
ends; that restless nervous energy; that dominant
individualism, working for good and for evil, and
withal that buoyancy and exuberance that comes
from freedom.

FREDERICK JACKSON TURNER
The Frontier in American History

It is my fate in this paper to swing constantly
from optimism to pessimism and back, but so is it the
fate of any one who writes or speaks of
anything in America—the most contradictory, the most
depressing, the most stirring, of any land in the
world today.

SINCLAIR LEWIS
Nobel Prize Acceptance Speech, 1930

... America, with all her wealth and power, has not yet produced a civilization good enough to satisfy the deepest wants of human creatures.

SINCLAIR LEWIS
Nobel Prize Acceptance Speech, 1930

Our country—this great Republic—means nothing unless it means the triumph of a real democracy, the triumph of popular government, and, in the long run, of an economic system under which each man shall be guaranteed the opportunity to show the best that there is in him.

THEODORE ROOSEVELT
"The New Nationalism"

Providence, that watches over children,
    drunkards, and fools
With silent miracles and other esoterica,
Continue to suspend the ordinary rules
And take care of the United States of
    America!

ARTHUR GUITERMAN
"Prayer," Gaily the Troubadour

One of the distinctive traits of the American people which the foreign visitor remarks is the prevailing democratic-folksy spirit. In contrast to some other countries, class consciousness among higher ranking persons is weak if not absent. People are not ashamed of a humble origin, but rather tend to be proud of it if they have made headway in life.

ÖMER CELÂL SARC
in As Others See Us

This America of everyday life is simple and accessible, though not discerned from Europe. It is a modern land where technical ingenuity is apparent

at every point, in the equipment of a kitchen
as well as of a car, but at the same time a land
of gardens, of flowers, of home activities, where a man
arriving from his office or his work-place, enjoys
tinkering at his bench, making a piece of furniture,
repainting his house, repairing a fence, or
mowing a lawn.

JACQUES FREYMOND
in As Others See Us

The American secret became open to me, after a
while, and I applied it to everything: all things were
to be produced with the least effort for the comfort
and satisfaction of the largest number of people.

LUIGI BARZINI, JR.
in As Others See Us

To watch an American on a beach, or crowding
into a subway, or buying a theater ticket, or sitting
at home with his radio on, tells you something
about one aspect of the American character:
the capacity to withstand a great deal of outside
interference, so to speak; a willing acceptance of a
frenzy which, though it's never self-conscious,
amounts to a willingness to let other people have and
assert their own lively, and even offensive character.
They are a tough race in this.

ALISTAIR COOKE
One Man's America

We are as rootless as so many traveling salesmen
living out of suitcases in cheap hotels, and are so
committed to thinking that change means progress
that we alter the shape of America as rapidly and as
completely as a demented child, wildly shaking a
kaleidoscope, changes its patterns.

JOHN KEATS
The New Romans

America was not planned; it became. Plans made
for it fell apart, were forgotten. From being a
polyglot nation, Americans became the worst linguists
in the world.

JOHN STEINBECK
America and Americans

America did not exist. Four centuries of work, of
bloodshed, of loneliness and fear created this land.
We built America and the process made us Americans—
a new breed, rooted in all races, stained and tinted
with all colors, a seeming ethnic anarchy.
Then in a little, little time, we became more alike
than we were different—a new society; not great,
but fitted by our very faults for greatness,
E Pluribus Unum.

JOHN STEINBECK
America and Americans

"I am a man, I am a horse; I am a team," cried one
voice; "I can whip any man in all Kentucky, by God!"
"I am an alligator," cried the other; "half-man,
half horse; can whip any man on the Mississippi by
God!" "I am a man," shouted the first; "have the
best horse, best dog, best gun and handsomest wife in all
Kentucky, by God!" "I am a Mississippi snapping-turtle,"
rejoined the second; "have bear's claws, alligator's
teeth, and the devil's tail; can whip any man, by God!"

reported by Henry Adams in The United States in 1800

America is closer to the year 2000 than anywhere
else on earth.

DAVID FROST
House Beautiful, *February 1971*

Americans can afford to experiment.

MAURICE SENDAK
House Beautiful, *February 1971*

Making allowances for human imperfections, I do
feel that, in America, the development of the
individual and his creative powers is possible, and
that, to me, is the most valuable asset in life.
In some countries men have neither political rights nor
the opportunity for free intellectual development.
But for most Americans such a situation would be
intolerable.

ALBERT EINSTEIN

In Britain, one of the minor duties of good
citizenship is not to disturb the private life of
other citizens. In this country, it's the other way
around—not to disturb other citizens who are enjoying
their private life in public.

ALISTAIR COOKE
One Man's America

Any well-established village in New England or
the northern Middle West could afford a town
drunkard, a town atheist, and a few Democrats.

DENIS W. BROGAN
The American Character

To be not only a best-seller in America but to be
really beloved, a novelist must assert that all
American men are tall, handsome, rich, honest, and
powerful at golf; that all country towns are filled
with neighbors who do nothing from day to day
save go about being kind to one another; that although
American girls may be wild, they change always into
perfect wives and mothers; and that, geographically,
America is composed solely of New York, which is
inhabited entirely by millionaires; of the
West, which keeps unchanged all the boisterous
heroism of 1870; and of the South, where every one

99

lives on a plantation perpetually glossy with moonlight
and scented with magnolias.

SINCLAIR LEWIS
Nobel Prize Acceptance Speech, 1930

I have often inquired of myself, what great principle
or idea it was that kept this confederacy so long
together. It was not the mere matter of the
separation of the colonies from the mother land;
but something in that Declaration giving liberty, not
alone to the people of this country, but hope to
the world for all future time. It was that which gave
promise that in due time the weights should be
lifed from the shoulders of all men, and that *all* should
have an equal chance. This is the sentiment embodied
in that Declaration of Independence.

ABRAHAM LINCOLN
Address at Independence Hall, Philadelphia, February 22, 1861

America! America! God mend thy every flaw,
Confirm thy soul in self-control, thy liberty in law.

KATHERINE LEE BATES
"America, The Beautiful"

19. Minorities

"Mister Rabbit, Mister Rabbit, your coat's
    mighty grey."
"Yes, bless God, been out 'fo' day."
    Ev'ry little soul gwine-a shine, shine,
    Ev'ry little soul gwine-a shine along.

"Mister Rabbit, Mister Rabbit, your ears mighty
   long."
"Yes, bless God, been put on wrong."
   Ev'ry little soul gwine-a shine, shine,
   Ev'ry little soul gwine-a shine along.

AMERICAN FOLK SONG
"Mister Rabbit"

━━━━━━━━

At the beginning of the World Series of 1947, I
experienced a completely new emotion, when the
National Anthem was played. This time, I thought,
it is being played for me, as much as for everyone
else. This is organized major league baseball, and I
am standing here with all the others; and everything
that takes place includes me.

JACKIE ROBINSON
This I Believe

━━━━━━━━

No, I'm not an American. I'm one of the 22 million
black people who are the victims of
Americanism. One of the 22 million black people
who are the victims of democracy, nothing but
disguised hypocrisy.

MALCOLM X
"The Ballot or The Bullet"

━━━━━━━━

We are a distinct cultural group, proud of our
culture and our institutions, and simply want to be
left alone to lead our good, black lives. In the new
world, as in this one, I want to be known,
not as a man who happens to be black,
but as a black man.

JULIUS LESTER
Look Out, Whitey! Black Power's Gon' Get Your Mama

━━━━━━━━

This is a theatre of assault. The play that will
split the heavens for us will be called THE

101

DESTRUCTION OF AMERICA. The heroes will be
Crazy Horse, Denmark Vesey, Patrice Lumumba, and
not history, not memory, not sad sentimental groping
for a warmth in our despair; these will be new men,
new heroes, and their enemies most of you
who are reading this.

LEROI JONES
"The Revolutionary Theater"
in Now and Tomorrow

No more auction block for me, no more, no more.
No more auction block for me, many thousand gone.

CIVIL WAR SONG

Sometimes it's like a hair across your cheek.
You can't see it, you can't find it with your fingers,
but you keep brushing at it because the feel
of it is irritating.

MARIAN ANDERSON
in "My Life in a White World" by Emily Kimbrough,
Ladies' Home Journal, September 1960

The fear I heard in my father's voice . . . when he
realized that I really *believed* I could do anything
a white boy could do, and had every intention of proving
it, was not at all like the fear I heard when one of
us was ill or had fallen down the stairs or strayed
too far from the house. It was another fear, a fear
that the child, in challenging the white world's
assumptions, was putting himself in the path of
destruction.

JAMES BALDWIN
The Fire Next Time

If you're white, you're right,
If you're black, stay back.

BLACK AMERICAN SAYING

Time will draw a veil over the white and black
in this hemisphere, and future generations will look
back upon the record of strife as it stands revealed
in the history of the people of this New World of ours
with wonder and incredulity. For they will not
understand the issue that the quarrel was about.

BRANCH RICKEY
quoted by Gerald Holland in The Realm of Sport

For three centuries, men of vastly different ways of life
have come to America, left behind their old language,
their old attachments to land and river, their betters
and their subordinates, their kin and their icons, and
have learned to speak and walk, to eat and trust,
in a new fashion.

MARGARET MEAD
New Lives for Old

In the third generation, the descendants of the
immigrants confronted each other, and knew they were
both Americans, in the same dress, with the same
language, using the same artifacts, troubled by the
same things, but they voted differently, had different
ideas about education and sex, and were still, in many
essential ways, as different from one another as their
grandfathers had been.

NATHAN GLAZER and DANIEL PATRICK MOYNIHAN
Beyond the Melting Pot

We cannot be satisfied until all our people have
equal opportunities for jobs, for homes, for education,
for health, and for political expression, and until all our
people have equal protection under the law.

HARRY S TRUMAN
Special Message to Congress, February 2, 1948

You cannot become thorough Americans-it you
think of yourselves in groups. America does not consist

of groups. A man who thinks of himself as belonging
to a particular national group in America has not yet
become an American, and the man who goes among
you to trade upon your nationality is no worthy
son to live under the Stars and Stripes.

WOODROW WILSON
May 10, 1915

⸻

We conclude that in the field of public education
the doctrine of "separate but equal" has no place.
Separate educational facilities are inherently unequal.

THE UNITED STATES SUPREME COURT
Brown vs. Board of Education of Topeka, 1954

⸻

On the Lower East Side in the early years of this
century we came as close to any guarantee as life
has ever offered. The guarantee was if you worked
hard, went to school, studied and saved, you could
participate in America.

HARRY GOLDEN

⸻

America is God's Crucible, the great Melting-Pot
where all the races of Europe are melting and re-forming!

ISRAEL ZANGWILL
The Melting Pot

⸻

I swear to the Lord
I still can't see
Why Democracy means
Everybody but me.

LANGSTON HUGHES
"The Black Man Speaks"

⸻

Black Power is an often implicit and often explicit
belief in black separatism. . . . Few ideas

104

are more unrealistic. There is no salvation for
the Negro through isolation.

MARTIN LUTHER KING, JR.

Every shut eye ain't asleep.

BLACK AMERICAN PROVERB

Lord, I've been down so long,
Down don't worry me.

BLACK AMERICAN SPIRITUAL

Well, I *was* and yet I was invisible, that was the
fundamental contradiction. I was and yet I was unseen.

RALPH ELLISON
The Invisible Man

America is so rich and fat, because it has eaten the
tragedy of millions of immigrants.

MICHAEL GOLD
Jews Without Money

One ever feels his twoness, an American, a Negro;
two souls, two thoughts, the two unreconciled strivings;
two warring ideals in one dark body, whose dogged
strength alone keeps it from being torn asunder.

W. E. B. DU BOIS
The Souls of the Black Folk

Life is to be lived, not controlled; and humanity is
won by continuing to play in face of certain
defeat. Our fate is to become one, and yet many—this
is not prophecy, but description. Thus one of the
greatest jokes in the world is the spectacle of the
whites busy escaping blackness and becoming blacker

every day, and the blacks striving toward whiteness, becoming quite dull and gray. None of us seems to know who he is or where he's going.

RALPH ELLISON
The Invisible Man

American Indians . . . had no knowledge that other varieties of mankind might exist. Usually an Indian group called itself simply "the people."

PETER FARB
Man's Rise to Civilization as Shown
by The Indians of North America

Going back as far as I can remember as a child in an Indian community, I had no sense of knowing about the other people around me except that we were all somehow equal. . . . Nobody was interested in getting on top of anybody else.

WILFRED PELLETIER
This Book Is About Schools

Black Power is not anti-white people, but is anti anything and everything that serves to oppress. If whites align themselves on the side of oppression, then Black Power must be anti-white. That, however, is not the decision of Black Power.

JULIUS LESTER
Look Out, Whitey! Black Power's Gon' Get Your Mama

The Negro says, "Now." Others say, "Never." The voice of responsible Americans . . . says, "Together." There is no other way. Until justice is blind to color, until education is unaware of race, until opportunity is unconcerned with the color of men's skins, emancipation will be a proclamation but not a fact.

LYNDON B. JOHNSON
Memorial Day Address, Gettysburg, Pennsylvania,
May 30, 1963

Brother, listen to what we say. There was a time when our forefathers owned this great island. Their seats extended from the rising to the setting sun. The Great Spirit had made it for the use of Indians. He had created the buffalo, the deer, and other animals for food. He had made the bear and the beaver. Their skins served us for clothing. He had scattered them over the country and taught us how to take them. He had caused the earth to produce corn for bread. All this he had done for His red children because He loved them. If we had some disputes about our hunting-ground they were generally settled without the shedding of much blood.

But an evil day came upon us. Your forefathers crossed the great water and landed on this island. Their numbers were small. They found friends and not enemies. They told us they had fled from their own country for fear of wicked men and had come here to enjoy their religion. They asked for a small seat. We took pity on them, granted their request, and they sat down among us. We gave them corn and meat; they gave us poison in return.

RED JACKET
Indian Warrior,
Speech at Council of Chiefs of the Six Nations, 1805

Whenever I hear anyone arguing for slavery, I feel a strong impulse to see it tried on him personally.

ABRAHAM LINCOLN
Speech to an Indiana Regiment, March 17, 1865

It is cheaper to feed the Indians than to fight them.

WILLIAM HENRY HARRISON
in William Henry Harrison, a Political Biography
by Dorothy B. Goebel

20. The Voice of the President

But the President represents all the people and must
face up to all the problems. He must be responsible,
as he sees it, for the welfare of every citizen and must
be sensitive to the will of every group. He cannot pick
and choose his issues. They all come with the job.

LYNDON B. JOHNSON
The Vantage Point

We do not distrust the future of essential democracy.
The people of the United States have not failed. In their
need they have registered a mandate that they
want direct, vigorous action.

They have asked for discipline and direction under
leadership. They have made me the present instrument
of their wishes. In the spirit of the gift I take it.

FRANKLIN D. ROOSEVELT
Inaugural Address, March 4, 1933

We stand today on the edge of a new frontier—
the frontier of the 1960's—a frontier of unknown
opportunities and perils—a frontier of unfulfilled
hopes and threats.

JOHN F. KENNEDY
Speech accepting Presidential nomination, July 15, 1960

I know that when things don't go well they like
to blame the Presidents, and that is one of the things
which Presidents are paid for. . . .

JOHN F. KENNEDY
News conference, June 14, 1962

Though, in reviewing the incidents of my administration, I am unconscious of intentional error, I am, nevertheless, too sensible of my defects, not to think it probable that I may have committed many errors. Whatever they may be, I fervently beseech the Almighty to avert or mitigate the evils to which they may tend. I shall also carry with me the hope that my country will never cease to view them with indulgence.

GEORGE WASHINGTON
Farewell Address, September 19, 1796

Oh, that lovely title, ex-President.

DWIGHT D. EISENHOWER
New York Post, *October 26, 1959*

There are no easy matters that will ever come to you as President. If they are easy, they will be settled at a lower level.

DWIGHT D. EISENHOWER
quoted by John F. Kennedy, December 17, 1962

County judge, chairman of a committee, President of the United States; they are all the same kind of jobs. It is the business of dealing with people.

HARRY S TRUMAN
in The Man of Independence *by Jonathan Daniels*

I'm glad to be rid of it. One really can't enjoy being President of the greatest republic in the history of the world. It's just too big a job for any one man to control it.

HARRY S TRUMAN
News reports of July 12, 1955

I would only hope that in these next four years we can so conduct ourselves in this country and so meet our responsibilities in the world in building peace in the

world that years from now people will look back
to the generation of the nineteen seventies and
how we've conducted ourselves and they will say,
God Bless America.

RICHARD M. NIXON
Election night speech, November 7, 1972

The people cannot look to legislation generally for
success. Industry, thrift, character, are not conferred
by act or resolve. Government cannot relieve
from toil. It can provide no substitute for the rewards
of service. It can, of course, care for the defective
and recognize distinguished merit. The normal must
care for themselves. Self-government means self-support.

CALVIN COOLIDGE
Have Faith in Massachusetts

Members of the Congress, the Constitution makes us
not rivals for power but partners for progress. We are
all trustees for the American people, custodians of the
American heritage. It is my task to *report* the state of the
Union—to *improve* it is the task of us all.

JOHN F. KENNEDY
State of the Union Message, January 11, 1962

No one can worship God or love his neighbor
on an empty stomach.

WOODROW WILSON
Speech, May 23, 1912

Liberty does not consist in mere declarations of the
rights of man. It consists in the translation of
those declarations into definite actions.

WOODROW WILSON
Address, July 4, 1914

But the right is more precious than peace, and we shall fight for the things which we have always carried nearest our hearts—for democracy, for the right of those who submit to authority to have a voice in their own Governments, for the rights and liberties of small nations, for a universal dominion of right by such a concert of free peoples as shall bring peace and safety to all nations and make the world itself at last free.

WOODROW WILSON
War Message to Congress, April 2, 1917

I wish to preach, not the doctrine of ignoble ease, but the doctrine of the strenuous life.

THEODORE ROOSEVELT
Speech, April 10, 1899

I stand for the square deal. But when I say that I am for the square deal, I mean not merely that I stand for fair play under the present rules of the game, but that I stand for having those rules change so as to work for a more substantial equality of opportunity and of reward for equally good service.

THEODORE ROOSEVELT
The New Nationalism

Fellow-citizens, *we* cannot escape history. . . . We —even *we* here—hold the power, and bear the responsibility. In *giving* freedom to the *slave*, we *assure* freedom to the *free*—honorable alike in what we give, and what we preserve. We shall nobly save, or meanly lose, the last best, hope of earth. Other means may succeed; this could not fail. The way is plain, peaceful, generous, just—a way which, if followed, the world will forever applaud, and God must forever bless.

ABRAHAM LINCOLN
Annual Message to Congress, December 1, 1862

Surely if the United States have a right to make war, they have a right to prevent it.

JAMES MONROE
Message to Congress, May 4, 1822

I repair, then, fellow-citizens, to the post you have assigned me. With experience enough in subordinate offices to have seen the difficulties of this, the greatest of all, I have learned to expect that it will rarely fall to the lot of imperfect man, to retire from this station with the reputation and the favor which bring him into it.

THOMAS JEFFERSON
First Inaugural Address, March 4, 1801

I claim not to have controlled events, but confess plainly that events have controlled me.

ABRAHAM LINCOLN

My movements to the chair of government will be accompanied by feelings not unlike those of a culprit, who is going to the place of his execution.

GEORGE WASHINGTON
Letter to Henry Knox, *April 1, 1789*

Giving up power is hard. But I would urge all of you, as leaders of this country, to remember that the truly revered leaders in world history are those who gave power to people, not those who took it away.

RICHARD M. NIXON
State of the Union Message, January 22, 1971

In every dark hour of our national life a leadership of frankness and vigor has met with that understanding and support of the people themselves which is essential to victory.

FRANKLIN D. ROOSEVELT
Inaugural Address, March 4, 1933

The President must be greater than anyone else,
but not better than anyone else. We subject him and
his family to close and constant scrutiny and denounce
them for things that we ourselves do every day. . . . We
give the President more work than a man can do, more
responsibility than a man should take, more pressure
than a man can bear. We advise him often and rarely
praise him. We wear him out, use him up, eat him up.
And with all this, Americans have a love for the
President that goes beyond loyalty or party nationality;
he is ours, and we exercise the right to destroy him.

JOHN STEINBECK
America and Americans

VII

"The People Will Live On"

21. The People

The people will live on.
The learning and blundering people will live on.
They will be tricked and sold and again sold
And go back to the nourishing earth for rootholds.

CARL SANDBURG
"The People, Yes"

. . . People are sometimes darn fools . . . they can
say silly, foolish, passionate or harsh things without
the slightest intent of acting on their words.

SAM J. ERVIN
The New York Times, *June 21, 1971*

The public has neither shame nor gratitude.

WILLIAM HAZLITT
Characteristics

The public is merely a multiplied "me."

MARK TWAIN

Bowed by the weight of centuries he leans
Upon his hoe and gazes on the ground,
The emptiness of ages in his face,
And on his back the burden of the world.

EDWIN MARKHAM
"The Man with the Hoe"

Two things only the people anxiously desire—
bread and circus games.

JUVENAL
Satires

The question is not whether the people agree with
the President or the Congress in this or that particular
decision, but whether, over the long run, the people
really get their way, have the final say.

CARL COHEN
The New York Times, *November 4, 1970*

That great enemy of reason, virtue, and religion,
the Multitude, that numerous piece of monstrosity.

SIR THOMAS BROWNE
Religio Medici

It is an easy and vulgar thing to please the mob . . .
but to improve them is a work fraught with difficulty,
and teeming with danger.

C. C. COLTON
Lacon

The great masses of the people . . . will more easily
fall victims to a great lie than to a small one.

ADOLF HITLER
Mein Kampf

Who is the Forgotten Man? He is the clean, quiet,
virtuous, domestic citizen who pays his debts and his
taxes and is never heard of out of his little circle. . . .
The Forgotten Man . . . delving away in patient industry,
supporting his family, paying his taxes, casting his vote,
supporting the church and the school. . . . He is the only
one for whom there is no provision in the great scramble

and the big divide. Such is the Forgotten Man. He works, he votes, generally he prays—but his chief business in life is to pay.

WILLIAM GRAHAM SUMNER
The Forgotten Man, 1883

Education makes a people easy to lead, but difficult to drive; easy to govern, but impossible to enslave.

LORD BROUGHAM
Address to the House of Commons, 1828

The mass of men lead lives of quiet desperation. What is called resignation is confirmed desperation.

HENRY DAVID THOREAU
Walden

The people are a many-headed beast.

ALEXANDER POPE
Imitations of Horace

The crowd is always caught by appearance and the crowd is all there is in the world.

MACHIAVELLI
The Prince

Wherever there is a crowd there is untruth.

SÖREN KIERKEGAARD

Those who try to lead the people can only do so by following the mob.

OSCAR WILDE

22. Prejudice and Tolerance

No man can thoroughly participate in any culture
unless he has been brought up and has lived according
to its forms, but he can grant to other cultures the same
significance to their participants which he
recognizes in his own.

RUTH BENEDICT
Patterns of Culture

Though all society is founded on intolerance, all
improvement is founded on tolerance.

GEORGE BERNARD SHAW
Preface, Saint Joan

Differing from a man in doctrine was no reason
why you should pull his house about his ears.

SAMUEL JOHNSON
in Journal of a Tour to the Hebrides,
by James Boswell, August 19, 1773

We fear things in proportion to our ignorance of them.

LIVY
History

It does me no injury for my neighbor to say there
are twenty Gods or no God!

THOMAS JEFFERSON

Men of genius are rarely much annoyed by the company of vulgar people, because they have a power of looking at such persons as objects of another race altogether.

SAMUEL TAYLOR COLERIDGE
Table Talk

We are none of us tolerant in what concerns us deeply and entirely.

SAMUEL TAYLOR COLERIDGE

Prejudices are the props of civilization.

ANDRÉ GIDE
The Counterfeiters

Our society is so constituted that most people remain all their lives in the condition in which they were born, and have to depend on their imagination for their notions of what it is like to be in the opposite condition.

GEORGE BERNARD SHAW
Preface, Too True to be Good

A man without force, is without the essential dignity of humanity. Human nature is so constituted, that it cannot honor a helpless man, although it can pity him.

FREDERICK DOUGLASS

Experience proves that those are oftenest abused who can be abused with the greatest impunity. Men are whipped oftenest who are whipped easiest.

FREDERICK DOUGLASS

Whose foot is to be the measure to which ours are all to be cut or stretched?

THOMAS JEFFERSON
Letter to M. N. G. Dufief, *April 19, 1814*

The true Islam has shown me that a blanket indictment
of all white people is as wrong as when whites make
blanket indictments against blacks.

Yes, I have been convinced that *some* American
whites do want to help cure the rampant racism
which is on the path to *destroying* this country.

MALCOLM X
Autobiography

I am a man; I deem nothing human alien to me.

TERENCE
Heautontimorumenos

Of Equality—as if it harm'd me, giving others the
same chances and rights
as myself—as if it were not
indispensable to my own rights
that others possess the same.

WALT WHITMAN
Leaves of Grass

23. Liberty and Freedom

What then is the spirit of liberty? I cannot define it;
I can only tell you my own faith. The spirit of liberty
is the spirit which is not too sure that it is right.
The spirit of liberty is the spirit which seeks to
understand the minds of other men and women.
The spirit of liberty is the spirit which weighs their
interests alongside its own without bias.

LEARNED HAND
I Am An American Day Speech, 1944

'Tis the gift to be simple, 'tis the gift to be free,
'Tis the gift to come down where we ought to be,
And when we find ourselves in the place just right
'Twill be in the valley of love and delight.
When true simplicity is gained,
To bow and to bend we will not be ashamed.
To turn, to turn will be our delight,
And by turning, turning we come 'round right.

ANN LEE
Shaker hymn,
"Simple Gifts"

I would say there are two basic complaints by
prisoners about prison. First: the monotony of prison
routine. Second: the numerous ways you are made
to feel you are finished as a man.

WILLIAM R. COONS
writer, English instructor, and former inmate at
Attica State Correctional Facility,
The New York Times Magazine, *October 10, 1971*

And ye shall know the truth, and the truth shall
make you free.

JOHN 8:32

There comes a point when too much freedom,
particularly freedom to choose from an almost
unlimited set of alternatives, becomes incapacitating
and paralyzing.

SEYMOUR L. HALLECK
"Why They'd Rather Do Their Own Thing,"
Think *Magazine, 1968*

The basic test of freedom is perhaps less in what we
are free to do than in what we are free not to do.

ERIC HOFFER

He is free who knows how to keep in his own hand
the power to decide, at each step, the course of his life,
and who lives in a society which does not block
the exercise of that power.

SALVADOR DE MADARIAGA

No one can be perfectly free till all are free; no one
can be perfectly moral till all are moral; no one can be
perfectly happy till all are happy.

HERBERT SPENCER
Social Statics

... We look forward to a world founded upon four
essential freedoms. The first is freedom of speech and
expression—everywhere in the world. The second is
freedom of every person to worship God in his own
way—everywhere in the world. The third is
freedom from want . . . everywhere in the world. The
fourth is freedom from fear . . . anywhere in the world.

FRANKLIN D. ROOSEVELT
Speech, January 6, 1941

"Freedom from fear" could be said to sum up
the whole philosophy of human rights.

DAG HAMMARSKJÖLD
Address, May 20, 1956

Once freedom lights its beacon in a man's heart,
the gods are powerless against him.

JEAN-PAUL SARTRE
The Flies

Oh, freedom! Oh, freedom!
Oh, freedom over me!
An' before I'd be a slave,

123

I'll be buried in my grave,
An' go home to my Lord an' be free.

BLACK AMERICAN SPIRITUAL
"Oh, Freedom"

Handcuffs
Have steel fangs
Whose bite is more painful
Than a whole battalion
Of fleas.

OSWALD JOSEPH MTSHALI,
Sounds of a Cowhide Drum,
The New York Times, *June 20, 1971*

. . . The most precious freedom secured to the
individual by our Constitution is the privacy of his
mind, the freedom of his thought and the sanctity of
his conscience.

SAM J. ERVIN
The New York Times, *June 21, 1971*

. . . One of the most fragile of our assets, our freedom.

ROGER WILKINS
The New York Times, *December 22, 1970*

Why did I choose to make this leap into the West—
into, if not the unknown, at any rate a great deal of
uncertainty?
The simple answer is: Because I want to be free—
free to dance as I please, free to develop my art,
free to work with whom I want to work, free to make the
maximum use of all the talents nature has
provided me with.

NATALYA MAKAROVA
*Russian-born ballerina who defected from
Leningrad Kirov Ballet in London,*
New York Post, *January 2, 1971*

124

Is life so dear or peace so sweet as to be purchased
at the price of chains and slavery? Forbid it, Almighty
God. I know not what course others may take,
but as for me, give me liberty or give me death!

PATRICK HENRY
Address to the Virginia Convention, March 1775

The first principle of a free society is an untrammeled
flow of words in an open forum.

ADLAI E. STEVENSON
The New York Times, *January 19, 1962*

The basis of our governments being the opinion of the
people, the very first object should be to keep that right;
and were it left to me to decide whether we should have
a government without newspapers, or newspapers
without a government, I should not hesitate a moment
to prefer the latter.

THOMAS JEFFERSON
Letter, January 16, 1787

Freedom of the press is not an end in itself but a
means to the end of a free society.

FELIX FRANKFURTER
The New York Times, *November 28, 1954*

If all mankind minus one, were of one opinion, and
only one person were of the contrary opinion, mankind
would be no more justified in silencing that one person,
than he, if he had the power, would be justified in
silencing mankind.

JOHN STUART MILL
On Liberty

Liberty means responsibility. That is why
most men dread it.

GEORGE BERNARD SHAW
Maxims for Revolutionists

125

When an American says he loves his country, he
means not only that he loves the New England
hills, the prairies glistening in the sun or the wide
rising plains, the mountains and the seas. He means
that he loves an inner air, an inner light in which
freedom lives and in which a man can draw the
breath of self-respect.

ADLAI E. STEVENSON
Time, *September 8, 1952*

It is the nature of slavery to render its victims
so abject that at last, fearing to be free, they multiply
their own chains. You can liberate a freeman, but you
cannot liberate a slave.

LOUIS J. HALLE

This will remain the land of the free only so
long as it is the home of the brave.

ELMER DAVIS
But We Were Born Free

If we are ever elevated, our elevation will have
been accomplished through our own instrumentality. . . .
No people that has been solely dependent upon foreign
aid, or rather, upon the efforts of those in any way
identified with the oppressor, to undo the heavy burdens,
ever stood forth in the attitude of freedom.

FREDERICK DOUGLASS

"How does it feel to be free?" she asked.
"I like it," said Wilbur. "That is, I guess I like it."
Actually, Wilbur felt queer to be outside his fence,
with nothing between him and the big world.

E. B. WHITE
Charlotte's Web

24. Law and Justice

Public opinion's always in advance of the Law.
JOHN GALSWORTHY
Windows

Law is merely the expression of the will of the strongest for the time being, and therefore laws have no fixity, but shift from generation to generation.
HENRY ADAMS
The Law of Civilization and Decay

The law, so far as it depends on learning, is indeed, as it has been called, the government of the living by the dead. To a very considerable extent no doubt it is inevitable that the living should be so governed.... But the present has a right to govern itself so far as it can; and it ought always to be remembered that historic continuity with the past is not a duty, it is only a necessity.
OLIVER WENDELL HOLMES
The Mind and Faith of Justice Holmes

We are under a Constitution, but the Constitution is what the judges say it is.
CHARLES EVANS HUGHES
Speech, Elmira, New York, May 3, 1907

Government can easily exist without law, but law
cannot exist without government.

BERTRAND RUSSELL
"Ideas That Have Helped Mankind," Unpopular Essays

The law is but words and paper without the hands
and swords of men.

JAMES HARRINGTON
The Commonwealth of Oceana

If it were not for injustice, men would not know justice.

HERACLITUS

The love of justice is simply, in the majority of men,
the fear of suffering injustice.

FRANÇOIS LA ROCHEFOUCAULD
Maxims

It may be true that the law cannot make a man love
me. But it can keep him from lynching me, and I
think that's pretty important.

MARTIN LUTHER KING, JR.
The Wall Street Journal, *November 13, 1962*

Where law ends, there tyranny begins.

WILLIAM PITT
Speech, January 9, 1770

In its beginnings law is a means toward the peaceable
ordering of society. It stands beside religion and
morality as one of the regulative agencies by which
men are restrained and the social interest in
general security is protected.

ROSCOE POUND
The Spirit of the Common Law

Laws and institutions must go hand in hand with
the progress of the human mind. As that becomes
more developed, more enlightened, as new discoveries
are made, new truths disclosed, and manners and
opinions change with the change of circumstances,
institutions must advance also, and keep pace with
the times. We might as well require a man to wear
still the coat which fitted him when a boy, as civilized
society to remain ever under the regime of their
barbarous ancestors.

THOMAS JEFFERSON
Letter, July 12, 1816

———————

Peace and justice are two sides of the same coin.

DWIGHT D. EISENHOWER
News conference, February 6, 1957

———————

I am describing the perceptions of some of the
residents of our ghettos and barrios, of our urban and
rural poor, of the economically and socially deprived.
These are people to whom the law may seem to be
both a mystery and an oppression; they are people
whose vaunted "day in court" may well consist of
a few minutes—or even a few seconds—before
an impatient judge in a dingy courtroom; people for
whom a plea or verdict of guilty is an inevitable
conclusion.

ARTHUR J. GOLDBERG
The New York Times, *April 12, 1971*

———————

To make laws that man cannot, and will not obey,
serves to bring all law into contempt.

ELIZABETH CADY STANTON
Address, 1861

———————

Law never made men a whit more just.

HENRY DAVID THOREAU
Civil Disobedience

129

The law, in its majestic equality, forbids all men to sleep under bridges, to beg in the streets, and to steal bread—the rich as well as the poor.

ANATOLE FRANCE
Crainquebille

Rigorous law is often rigorous injustice.

TERENCE
Heautontimorumenos

I know of no method to secure the repeal of bad or obnoxious laws so effective as their stringent execution.

ULYSSES S. GRANT
Inaugural Address, March 4, 1869

The best use of good laws is to teach men to trample bad laws under their feet.

WENDELL PHILLIPS
Speech, April 12, 1852

It is better that ten guilty persons escape than that one innocent suffer.

SIR WILLIAM BLACKSTONE
Commentaries

I submit that an individual who breaks a law that conscience tells him is unjust, and who willingly accepts the penalty of imprisonment in order to arouse the conscience of the community over its injustice, is in reality expressing the highest respect for law.

MARTIN LUTHER KING, JR.
Why We Can't Wait

Justice is like the kingdom of God—it is not without us as a fact, it is within us as a great yearning.

GEORGE ELIOT
Romola

25. Non-Violence and Violence

Who overcomes by force hath overcome but
half his foe.

JOHN MILTON
Paradise Lost

Nonviolence is a powerful and just weapon. It is a
weapon unique in history, which cuts without
wounding and enobles the man who wields it.
It is a sword that heals.

MARTIN LUTHER KING, JR.
Why We Can't Wait

I am for violence if non-violence means we continue
postponing a solution to the American black man's
problem—just to *avoid* violence I don't go for
non-violence if it also means a delayed solution.

MALCOLM X
Autobiography

And he who rejoices at the destruction of human
life is not fit to be entrusted with power in the world.

LAO-TSE
Tao Te Ching

In the old wars clutches of short swords and jabs
        into faces with spears.
In the new wars long-range guns and smashed walls,

guns running a spit of metal and men falling
in tens and twenties.
In the wars to come new silent deaths, new silent
hurlers not yet dreamed out in the heads of men.

CARL SANDBURG
"Wars"

If we take vengeance on vengeance, vengeance
will never end.

VIETNAMESE PROVERB

The hydrogen bomb is history's exclamation point.
It ends an age-long sentence of manifest violence.

MARSHALL MC LUHAN

For at the real heart of battle for equality is a deep
seated belief in the democratic process. Equality depends
not on the force of arms or tear gas but depends upon
the force of moral right—not on recourse to violence
but on respect for law and order.

LYNDON B. JOHNSON
Address to the Congress on Voting Rights, 1965

It is the melancholy law of human societies to be
compelled sometimes to choose a great evil in order
to ward off a greater; to deter their neighbors from rapine
by making it cost them more than honest gains.

THOMAS JEFFERSON
Letter to William Short, *November 28, 1814*

Might and Right are always fighting.
In our youth it seems exciting.
Right is always nearly winning.
Might can hardly keep from grinning.

CLARENCE DAY
"Might and Right"

I don't believe in violence for many reasons. I'm
just not prone to violence. I don't know what blowing
up the Bank of America does for a black child that's
starving in the ghetto; I don't know what it does for the
mother who has had a baby bitten by a rat and lives
under bad conditions and hasn't got enough
food for the family.

SAMMY DAVIS, JR.
The New York Times, *April 18, 1971*

It's got to be the ballot or the bullet. The ballot
or the bullet. If you're afraid to use an expression like
that, you should get on out of the country, you should
get back in the cotton patch, you should get
back in the alley.

MALCOLM X
"The Ballot or The Bullet"

Nonviolence is a weapon of the strong. With the weak
it might easily be hypocrisy. . . . My daily experience . . .
is that every problem lends itself to solution if we are
determined to make the law of truth and nonviolence
the law of life. For truth and nonviolence are, to me,
faces of the same coin.

MOHANDAS K. GANDHI
My Faith in Nonviolence

Not by might, nor by power, but by my spirit,
saith the Lord of Hosts.

ZECHARIAH 4:6

We regard men as infinitely precious and possessed
of unfulfilled capacities for reason, freedom, and
love. In affirming these principles we are aware of
countering perhaps the dominant conceptions of man in
the twentieth century: that he is a thing to be
manipulated, and that he is inherently incapable of

directing his own affairs. We oppose the
depersonalization that reduces human beings to the
status of things—if anything, the brutalities of the
twentieth century teach that means and ends are
intimately related, that vague appeals to "posterity"
cannot justify the mutilations of the present.

TOM HAYDEN

Address, Students for a Democratic Society,
"The Port Huron Statement," 1962

Gwine to lay down my sword and shield,
    down by the riverside,
Down by the riverside, down by the riverside,
Gwine to lay down my sword and shield,
    down by the riverside,
Ain't gwine study war no more.

BLACK AMERICAN SPIRITUAL

VIII

"The Root of All Evil"

26. Money

The lack of money is the root of all evil.

MARK TWAIN

For the love of money is the root of all evil: which while some coveted after, they have erred from the faith, and pierced themselves through with many sorrows.

I TIMOTHY 6:10

It's a kind of spiritual snobbery that makes people think they can be happy without money.

ALBERT CAMUS
Notebooks 1935–1942

Money is the most important thing in the world. It represents health, strength, honor, generosity and beauty as conspicuously and undeniably as the want of it represents illness, weakness, disgrace, meanness and ugliness. Not the least of its virtues is that it destroys base people as certainly as it fortifies and dignifies noble people.

GEORGE BERNARD SHAW
Preface, Major Barbara

O money, money, money, I'm
not necessarily one of those
who think thee holy,

But I often stop to wonder
how thou canst go out so
fast when thou comest in
so slowly.

OGDEN NASH
"Hymn to the Thing That Makes the Wolf Go"

The business of America is business.

CALVIN COOLIDGE
Speech, January 17, 1925

Modern man is alienated from himself, from his
fellow men, and from nature. He has been transformed
into a commodity, experiences his life forces as an
investment which must bring him the maximum profit
obtainable under existing market conditions.

ERICH FROMM
The Art of Loving

From each according to his abilities, to each
according to his needs.

KARL MARX
The Gotha Program

Surplus wealth is a sacred trust which its possessor
is bound to administer in his lifetime for the
good of the community.

ANDREW CARNEGIE
"Wealth,"
North American Review, *June 1889*

It is easier for a camel to go through the eye of a
needle, than for a rich man to enter into the
kingdom of God.

MATTHEW 19:24

The worst crime against working people is a company
which fails to operate at a profit.

SAMUEL L. GOMPERS

There are few sorrows, however poignant, in which
a good income is of no avail.

LOGAN PEARSALL SMITH
"Afterthoughts," All Trivia

There are only two families in the world, my old
grandmother used to say, the *Haves* and the *Have-nots.*

MIGUEL DE CERVANTES
Don Quixote

Certainly there are lots of things in life
    that money won't buy,
    but it's very funny—
Have you ever tried to buy them without money?

OGDEN NASH
"The Terrible People"

Never spend your money before you have it.
Never buy what you do not want, because it is cheap;
it will be dear to you.

THOMAS JEFFERSON
Letter, February 21, 1825

The propensity to truck, barter, and exchange . . . is
common to all men, and to be found in no other
race of animals.

ADAM SMITH
The Wealth of Nations

The happiest time in any man's life is when he is
in red-hot pursuit of a dollar with a reasonable
prospect of overtaking it.

JOSH BILLINGS

I was born into it and there was nothing I could do about it. It was there, like air or food or any other element. . . . The only question with wealth is what you do with it.

JOHN D. ROCKEFELLER, JR.

Time, *September 24, 1956*

Perhaps you will say a man is not young; I answer, he is rich; he is not gentle, handsome, witty, brave, good-humored, but he is rich, rich, rich, rich—that one word contradicts everything you say against him.

HENRY FIELDING

The Miser

It's the syme the whole world over,
'Tis the poor what gets the blyme,
While the rich 'as all the plysures.
Now ain't that a blinkin' shyme?

AMERICAN POPULAR SONG

Money is human happiness in the abstract: he, then, who is no longer capable of enjoying human happiness in the concrete devotes himself utterly to money.

ARTHUR SCHOPENHAUER

While there is flesh there is money—or the want of money; but money is always on the brain so long as there is a brain in reasonable order.

SAMUEL BUTLER

Notebooks

Wealth in modern societies is distributed according to opportunity; and while opportunity depends partly upon talent and energy, it depends still more upon

birth, social position, access to education and inherited
wealth; in a word, upon property.

RICHARD H. TAWNEY
The Acquisitive Society

Money is like manure. If you spread it around, it
does a lot of good. But if you pile it up in one place,
it stinks like hell.

CLINT MURCHISON, JR.
Time, *June 16, 1961*

When the farmer comes to town, with his wagon
    broken down,
Oh, the farmer is the man who feeds them all!
If you'll only look and see, I'm sure you will
    agree
That the farmer is the man who feeds them all!
The farmer is the man, the farmer is the man,
Lives on credit 'till the fall;
Then they take him by the hand, and they lead him
    from the land,
And the merchant is the man who gets it all.

AMERICAN FOLK SONG

That most delicious of all privileges—spending
other people's money.

JOHN RANDOLPH

Almost any man knows how to earn money, but not
one in a million knows how to spend it.

HENRY DAVID THOREAU

27. Poverty

What you gonna do when the meat's all gone, honey?
What you gonna do when the meat's all gone, babe?
What you gonna do when the meat's all gone?
Sit in the kitchen and gnaw on a bone
Honey, baby mine.

AMERICAN FOLK SONG
"The Crawdad Song"

Bedbugs are what people mean when they say:
Poverty.

MICHAEL GOLD
Jews Without Money

No man can be a good citizen unless he has a wage
more than sufficient to cover the bare cost of living,
and hours of labor short enough so that after his day's
work is done he will have time and energy to bear
his share in the management of the community, to help
in carrying the general load. We keep countless men
from being good citizens by the conditions of life
with which we surround them.

THEODORE ROOSEVELT
The New Nationalism

The poor man's wisdom is despised, and his
words are not heard.

ECCLESIASTES 9:16

'Leven cent cotton, forty cent meat,
How in the world can a poor man eat?
Flour up high, cotton down low,
How in the world can we raise the dough?
Our clothes worn out, shoes run down,
Old slouch hat with a hole in the crown.
Back nearly broken, fingers all wore out,
Cotton goin' down to rise no more.
'Leven cent cotton, forty cent meat,
Feels like a chain is on our feet.
Poor getting poorer all around here,
Kids coming regular ev'ry year;
Planted corn, was a wheat year;
Planted wheat and it turned a corn year.
No use talkin', any man's beat,
With 'leven cent cotton and forty cent meat.

BOB MILLER and EMMA DERMER
"Eleven Cent Cotton"

For ye have the poor always with you.

MATTHEW 26:11

The seven deadly sins. . . . Food, clothing, firing,
rent, taxes, respectability and children. Nothing can
lift those seven millstones from man's neck but money;
and the spirit cannot soar until the millstones are lifted.

GEORGE BERNARD SHAW
Major Barbara

A hungry man is not a free man.

ADLAI E. STEVENSON
Speech, September 6, 1952

An empty stomach is not a good political adviser.

ALBERT EINSTEIN
Cosmic Religion

A hungry people is unreasonable, unjust and unmerciful.

SENECA
"De Brevitate Vitae"

The hungry man does not hear.

SWAHILI PROVERB

Poverty destroys pride. It is difficult for an empty bag to stand upright.

ALEXANDRE DUMAS, FILS

But I soon got tired of third-class journeys
And dinners of bread and water;
So I fell in love with a rich attorney's
Elderly, ugly daughter.

WILLIAM S. GILBERT
Trial By Jury

How right the working classes are in their "materialism." How right they are to realize that the belly comes before the soul, not in the scale of values but in point of time.

GEORGE ORWELL

Poverty does not mean the absence of money. Poverty is a name for that condition of life that prevents a man from gaining the benefits of his own society and from fulfilling the possibilities that lie within him.

HAROLD TAYLOR
"The Frontiers of Education"

Two nations, between whom there is no intercourse and no sympathy; who are as ignorant of each other's

habits, thoughts, and feelings as if they were dwellers
in different zones, or inhabitants of different planets;
who are formed by different breeding, are fed by
different food, are ordered by different manners,
and are not governed by the same laws—
the rich and the poor.

BENJAMIN DISRAELI
Sybil

Until we attack poverty with all the expert weapons
that the latest advances in economics, sociology, and
politics have placed within our reach, we shall continue
to have a national system that gives 30,000,000 people
a life of such limited happiness, such cramping
limitations on personal development, and such exposure
to sudden onslaughts of fear, deprivation, and misery,
that we can expect from our people very little devotion
to country, little sense of solicitude for their fellowmen,
little expression even of right ethical feeling, and no
manifestations of philosophic wisdom, poetic grace, and
determined purpose as will give our national
life a higher meaning.

ALLAN NEVINS
"The Tradition of The Future,"
Saturday Review, *June 8, 1968*

Hunger allows no choice
To the citizen or the police;
We must love one another or die.

W. H. AUDEN

But the new poverty is constructed so as to destroy
aspiration; it is a system designed to be impervious
to hope. The other America does not contain the
adventurous seeking a new life and land. It is populated
by the failures, by those driven from the land and
bewildered by the city, by the old people suddenly

144

confronted with the torments of loneliness and poverty,
and by minorities facing a wall of prejudice.

MICHAEL HARRINGTON
The Other America

Poverty in the United States is a culture, an institution,
a way of life.

MICHAEL HARRINGTON
The Other America

It's a mighty hard row that my poor hands have hoed;
My poor feet have traveled a hot dusty road,
Out of your dust bowl and westward we rolled,
And your desert was hot and your mountain was cold.

WOODY GUTHRIE
"Pastures of Plenty"

Frequently, the deprived individual feels alienated,
not fully a part of society, left out, frustrated in what
he can do. This alienation is expressed in a ready
willingness to believe in the corruptness of leaders,
and a generally antagonistic feeling toward "big shots."

FRANK REISSMAN
The Culturally Deprived Child

East Harlem isn't a German camp. But it's worse.
Because in East Harlem the sun is shining and there's
not a gate or a lock or a machine-gun post. . . . I'm
beginning to feel that I'm in prison.

JULIUS HORWITZ
The Inhabitants

In buildings like this they'll steal your dirty
diapers. Find yourself a first-rate building. Just forget
that you're getting money on assistance. . . . Don't think
that you have to look at these holes just because you're

getting the money for free. It's not free. Nothing is for
free. Least of all the things that we think are free.

JULIUS HORWITZ
The Inhabitants

Look the next time you see a beggar. The successful
beggar always suggests he too is human. I don't know
why we should have beggars. But beggars beg you to
look on their face. And they are vicious when you turn
from their face. Almost like the anger of a god.

JULIUS HORWITZ
The Inhabitants

It is well known that the poor are more willing to give
than the rich. Nevertheless, poverty beyond a certain
point may make it impossible to give, and is so
degrading, not only because of the suffering it causes
directly, but because of the fact that it deprives the
poor of the joy of giving.

ERICH FROMM
The Art of Loving

I asked God, Where do the poor find rest?
Will they truly have rest? Tell me, oh God, what will
happen after death to a life that has been lived in
Martyrdom? You have said "Blessed are the poor, for
theirs is the kingdom of heaven." . . . I rebel, oh Lord,
not against Your holy purposes, but against what
people say about the poor.

OSCAR LEWIS
quoting a poor woman
in A Death in the Sanchez Family

Guadalupe died as she had lived, without medical
care, in unrelieved pain, in hunger, worrying about
how to pay the rent or raise money for the bus fare
for a trip to the hospital, working up to the last day of her

life at the various pathetic jobs she had to take to keep
going, leaving nothing of value but a few old religious
objects and the tiny rented space she had occupied.

OSCAR LEWIS
A Death in the Sanchez Family

The evil to be attacked is not sin, suffering, greed,
priestcraft, kingcraft, demagogy, monopoly, ignorance,
drink, war, pestilence, nor any of the other consequences
of poverty, but just poverty itself.

GEORGE BERNARD SHAW
Preface, Major Barbara

But poverty is not measured by history. It is measured
by the standards of a man's own community. If most
of America is well-fed, the man who can't find three
meals a day for his family is poor. If most of America
has modern weather-proof housing, the man whose
home is leaky and has no piped water is poor. If
most of America has enough medical care to stay alive
until age seventy, the man who can't afford to live
beyond age fifty-five is poor. Such a man is poor
statistically. But he is poor in a more damaging way:
he is a failure in his neighbor's eye and in his own.

BEN H. BAGDIKIAN
In the Midst of Plenty

28. Work

Work banishes those three great evils, boredom,
vice and poverty.

VOLTAIRE
Candide

The work that the kids saw around them was so
odious, so boring, so worthless that they came to regard
WORK as the only dirty four-letter word in the
English language.

ABBIE HOFFMAN
Woodstock Nation

The lady—bearer of this—says she has two sons who
want to work. Set them at it, if possible. Wanting
to work is so rare a merit, that it should be encouraged.

ABRAHAM LINCOLN
Letter to Major Ramsay, *October 17, 1861*

Efficiency of a practically flawless kind may be
reached naturally in the struggle for bread. But there
is something beyond—a higher point, a subtle and
unmistakable touch of love and pride beyond mere
skill; almost an inspiration which gives to all work
that finish what is almost art—which *is* art.

JOSEPH CONRAD

The test of a vocation is the love of the
drudgery it involves.

LOGAN PEARSALL SMITH

Monotony is the law of nature. Look at the monotonous
manner in which the sun rises. . . . The monotony
of necessary occupations is exhilarating and life-giving.

MOHANDAS K. GANDHI

We mean to make things over,
    we are tired of toil for naught,
With but bare enough to live upon
    and ne'er an hour for thought;
We want to feel the sunshine,
    and we want to smell the flow'rs,

We are sure that God has willed it,
   and we mean to have eight hours.
We're summoning our forces
   from the ship-yard, shop, and mill.

Eight hours for work, eight hours for rest,
Eight hours for what we will;
Eight hours for work, eight hours for rest,
Eight hours for what we will.

I. G. BLANCHARD
*labor movement song written
during campaign for eight-hour working day, 1868,
"Eight Hours"*

And what is it to work with love?

It is to weave the cloth
With threads
Drawn from your heart,
Even as if your beloved
Were to wear that cloth.

KAHLIL GIBRAN
The Prophet

It is better to have loafed and lost than
never to have loafed at all.

JAMES THURBER

Anyone can do any amount of work, provided it
isn't the work he is supposed to be doing at the moment.

ROBERT BENCHLEY

I studied the lives of great men and famous women;
and I found that the men and women who got to the
top were those who did the jobs they had in hand,
with everything they had of energy, enthusiasm
and hard work.

HARRY S TRUMAN

Happiness lies not in the mere possession of money; it
lies in the joy of achievement, in the thrill of
creative effort.

FRANKLIN D. ROOSEVELT
Inaugural Address, March 4, 1933

The crowning fortune of a man is to be born to some
pursuit which finds him employment and happiness,
whether it be to make baskets, or broadswords,
or canals, or statues, or songs.

RALPH WALDO EMERSON

Oh, why don't you work like other
    men do?
How the hell can I work when there's
    no work to do?
Hallelujah, I'm a bum,
    hallelujah, bum again,
Hallelujah, give us a handout
    to revive us again.

AMERICAN FOLK SONG
"Hallelujah, I'm a Bum"

But alas! My sense of elation did not last long.
To guide a team for a few minutes as an experiment
was one thing—to plow all day like a hired hand was
another. It was not a chore, it was a job. It meant
moving to and fro hour after hour, day after day, with
no one to talk to but the horses. It meant trudging
eight or nine miles in the forenoon and as many
more in the afternoon, with less than an hour off at
noon. . . . Neighbor Button said to my father in my
hearing, "That chap's too young to run a plow," a
judgment which pleased and flattered me greatly.

HAMLIN GARLAND
A Son of the Middle Border

Man becomes a "nine to fiver," he is part of the
labor force, or the bureaucratic force of clerks and
managers. He has little initiative, his tasks are prescribed
by the organization of the work; there is even little
difference between those high up on the ladder and
those on the bottom. They all perform tasks prescribed
by the whole structure of the organization, at a prescribed
speed, and in a prescribed manner.

ERICH FROMM
The Art of Loving

We stand today in danger of forgetting the use of our
hands. To forget how to dig the earth and tend the soil
is to forget ourselves.

MOHANDAS K. GANDHI
Speech, July 31, 1946

A man's work is one of the more important parts
of his social identity, of his self, indeed of the fate in
the one life he has to live, for there is something
almost irrevocable about the choice of occupation as
there is about the choice of a mate.

EVERETT HUGHES

How bravely all them collier lads, they toil
    beneath the ground,
Digging for the coal as do the days and nights
    go round;
And anxiously their fam'lies wait—how often
    it is said,
You never know by nightfall just how many might
    be dead.

ENGLISH FOLK SONG
"Down in a Coal Mine"

Hire yourself out to work which is beneath you
rather than become dependent on others.

THE TALMUD

The problem is people who work full-time jobs at part-time pay. Most of the poor people in our country are working every day and they're making wages so inadequate that they cannot even begin to function in the mainstream of the economic life of our nation. . . . But no labor is really menial unless you're not getting adequate wages. What makes it menial is the income, the wages.

MARTIN LUTHER KING, JR.
Address, March 8, 1968

I think that there is far too much work done in the world, that immense harm is caused by the belief that work is virtuous, and that what needs to be preached in modern industrial countries is quite different from what always has been preached.

BERTRAND RUSSELL

. . . Most work in our society is meaningless, degrading and inconsistent with self-realization. The new generation is not "lazy," and it is glad enough to put great effort into any work that is worthwhile.

CHARLES REICH
The Greening of America

After each fire in an apartment, or a business, I sit exhausted on the dark slate of tenement stoops, or at a cobblestoned curb. My nose walls are coated with soot, and I spit the black phlegm of my trade. I am only 31, but I feel 50. Men pass by and ask how I feel, but I just nod to them. I don't feel like speaking. I feel like I have climbed a mountain, and I bask in the silent personal satisfaction of victory.

DENNIS SMITH
Report From Engine Co. 82

It is not upon thee to finish the work; neither art thou free to abstain from it.

THE TALMUD

152

IX

"A Free Society"

29. The Governments of Man

My definition of a free society is a society where
it is safe to be unpopular.

ADLAI E. STEVENSON
Address, Detroit, October 1952

The sum of all known reverence I add up in
you whoever you are,
The President is there in the White House
for you,
it is not you who are here for him,
The Secretaries act in their bureaus for
you, not you here for them,
The Congress convenes every Twelfth-
month for you,
Laws, courts, the forming of States, the
charters of cities,
the going and coming of commerce and
mails, are all for you.

WALT WHITMAN
"A Song for Occupations," Leaves of Grass

Do the People, directly or indirectly, participate in
directing the policies of their government? If they do,
however wrongheaded their policies, they have a
democracy; if not, however wise the policies chosen for
them, they have none.

CARL COHEN
The New York Times, *November 4, 1970*

There is no telling to what extremes of cruelty and
ruthlessness a man will go when he is freed from the
fears, hesitations, doubts and the vague stirrings of
decency that go with individual judgment. When we
lose our individual independence in the corporateness
of a mass movement, we find a new freedom—freedom
to hate, bully, lie, torture, murder and betray without
shame and remorse.

ERIC HOFFER

A democrat need not believe that the majority will
always decide wisely; what he must believe is that the
decision of the majority, whether wise or unwise, must
be accepted until such time as the majority decides
otherwise.

BERTRAND RUSSELL
"Ideas That Have Harmed Mankind," Unpopular Essays

In the democracies non-conformity is possible and,
in fact, by no means entirely absent; in the totalitarian
systems, only a few unusual heroes and martyrs
can be expected to refuse obedience.

ERICH FROMM
The Art of Loving

Democracy was invented as a device for reconciling
government with liberty.

BERTRAND RUSSELL
"Ideas That Have Helped Mankind," Unpopular Essays

Nothing is more certain than the indispensable
necessity of government, and it is equally undeniable,
that whenever and however it is instituted, the people
must cede to it some of their natural rights, in order to
vest it with requisite powers.

JOHN JAY
The Federalist

We vote too much. We deliberate too little. We have brought within the scope of the federal jurisdiction a vast number of subjects that do not belong here, but are nevertheless here. What we need to do is to stop passing laws. We have enough laws now to govern the world for the next ten thousand years.

JAMES ALEXANDER REED
Speech, June 4, 1926

In a complex society, it is foolish to pretend that democracy is satisfied by a once-a-year election day. People must be able to "vote" every day by expressing their values on the job, as newly aware consumers, in many kinds of groups and organizations, and in a variety of public hearings.

CHARLES REICH
"Issues for a New Society,"
The New York Times, *March 9, 1971*

Some day we will come to realize that the right to food, shelter, and clothing at reasonable prices is as much an inalienable right as the right to life, liberty and the pursuit of happiness.

FIORELLO H. LA GUARDIA
The Making of an Insurgent

But what is government itself, but the greatest of all reflections on human nature? If men were angels, no government would be necessary. . . . In framing a government which is to be administered by men over men, the great difficulty lies in this: you must first enable the government to control the governed; and in the next place oblige it to control itself.

JAMES MADISON

Wherever the real power in a government lies, there is the danger of oppression. In our Government the real power lies in the majority of the community. . . .

JAMES MADISON

Shall we judge a country by the majority or by the minority? By the minority, surely.

RALPH WALDO EMERSON
"Considerations by the Way," Conduct of Life

There is only one sound argument for democracy, and that is the argument that it is a crime for any man to hold himself out as better than other men, and above all a most heinous offense for him to prove it.

H. L. MENCKEN
The Vintage Mencken

This, the Senate of the United States, is an odd, mixed place. It is hard and efficient, and it is soft and dawdling. It is harsh, and it is kind. It is dignity, and it is disorders. It is arrogant and it is humble. It believes in a kind of democracy . . . but it is in some things majestically undemocratic. It halts usurptions, and it usurps. It honors the system, and it rejects the system.

WILLIAM S. WHITE
Citadel: The Story of the U.S. Senate

This government, the offspring of our own choice, uninfluenced and unawed, adopted upon full investigation and mature deliberation, completely free in its principles, in the distribution of its powers, uniting security with energy, and containing within itself a provision for its own amendment, has a just claim to your confidence and your support.

GEORGE WASHINGTON
Farewell Address, September 19, 1796

The fact of the matter is that the experience of 20 years since the War shows that, even within the Communist empire, national interest has become more powerful than ideology, and that, when the chips are down,

Communist states are going to respond to their national interests rather than to the dictates of their ideology.

ARTHUR M. SCHLESINGER, JR.
in Playboy Interviews

No government is perfect. One of the chief virtues of a democracy, however, is that its defects are always visible and under democratic processes can be pointed out and corrected.

HARRY S TRUMAN

Sometimes it is said that man cannot be trusted with the government of himself. Can he, then, be trusted with the government of others? Or have we found angels in the form of kings to govern him? Let history answer this question.

THOMAS JEFFERSON
First Inaugural Address, March 4, 1801

The world will always be governed by self-interest. We should not try to stop this, we should try to make the self-interest of cads a little more coincident with that of decent people.

SAMUEL BUTLER
Notebooks

The majority *never* has right on its side. Never, I say! That is one of these social lies against which an independent, intelligent man must wage war. Who is it that constitute the majority of the population in a country? Is it the clever folk or the stupid? I don't imagine you will dispute the fact that at present the stupid people are in an absolutely overwhelming majority all the world over. But, good Lord!—you can never pretend that it is right that the stupid folk should govern the clever ones! Oh, yes—you can shout me down, I know! but you cannot

158

answer me. The majority has *might* on its side—
unfortunately; but *right* it has *not*. I am in the right—I and
a few other scattered individuals. The minority is always
in the right.

HENRIK IBSEN
An Enemy of the People

All government without the consent of the governed,
is the very definition of slavery.

JONATHAN SWIFT
Drapier's Letters

We hold these truths to be self-evident, that all men
are created equal, that they are endowed by their creator
with certain unalienable rights, that among these are
Life, Liberty, and the Pursuit of Happiness.

DECLARATION OF INDEPENDENCE

That all men are equal is a proposition to which, at
ordinary times, no sane individual has ever given his
assent.

ALDOUS HUXLEY
Proper Studies

He who confuses political liberty with freedom and
political equality with similarity has never thought for
five minutes about either.

GEORGE BERNARD SHAW
Maxims for Revolutionists

Dictators ride to and fro upon tigers which they dare
not dismount.

WINSTON S. CHURCHILL
While England Slept

All the ills of democracy can be cured by more democracy.

ALFRED E. SMITH
Speech, June 27, 1933

=====

The end of all political effort must be the well-being of the individual in a life of safety and freedom.

DAG HAMMARSKJÖLD
The New York Times, *October 18, 1960*

=====

While the Pobble was in the water some unidentified creatures came and ate his toes off, and when he got home his aunt remarked: It's a fact that the whole world knows, that Pobbles are happier without their toes, which is funny because it has a meaning, and one might even say a political significance. The whole theory of authoritarian government is summed up in the statement that Pobbles are happier without their toes.

GEORGE ORWELL

=====

The art of putting the right men in the right places is first in the science of government; but, that of finding places for the discontented is the most difficult.

TALLEYRAND

=====

Tyranny is always better organized than freedom.

CHARLES PÉGUY

=====

Democracy . . . is a condition where people believe that other people are as good as they are.

STUART CHASE

=====

". . . Are the Seven Commandments the same as they used to be, Benjamin?"

For once Benjamin consented to break his rule, and
he read out to her what was written on the wall. There
was nothing there now except a single Commandment.
It ran:

ALL ANIMALS ARE EQUAL
BUT SOME ANIMALS ARE MORE EQUAL
THAN OTHERS

After that it did not seem strange when next day the
pigs who were supervising the work of the farm all
carried whips in their trotters.

GEORGE ORWELL
Animal Farm

No one is fit to be trusted with power. . . . No one. . . .
Any man who has lived at all knows the follies and
wickedness he's capable of. If he does not know it, he
is not fit to govern others. And if he does know it, he
knows also that neither he nor any man ought to be
allowed to decide a single human fate.

C. P. SNOW

30. Politics

A statesman is an easy man,
He tells his lies by rote;
A journalist makes up his lies
And takes you by the throat;
So stay at home and drink your beer
And let the neighbors vote.

WILLIAM BUTLER YEATS
"The Old Stone Cross"

This is the first Convention of the space age—where a candidate can promise the moon and mean it.

DAVID BRINKLEY
Newsweek, *March 13, 1961*

═══════════

He serves his party best who serves the country best.

RUTHERFORD B. HAYES
Inaugural Address, March 5, 1877

═══════════

If you are goin' to cast your first vote next November and want to go into politics, do as I did. Get a followin', if it's only one man, and then go to the district leader and say: "I want to join the organization. I've got one man who'll follow me through thick and thin." The leader won't laugh at your one-man followin'. He'll shake your hand warmly, offer to propose you for membership in his club, take you down to the corner for a drink and ask you to call again.

GEORGE WASHINGTON PLUNKITT

═══════════

Politics means the art of compromise. Most politicians are all-too-well schooled in this art. They compromise to get nominated; they compromise to get elected; and they compromise time and time again, after they are elected, to stay in office.

DICK GREGORY
"Why I Want to Be President," Write Me In!

═══════════

The hard truth is that while most of the world's political leaders profess democracy as an ideal, they do not support or practice it. Its practice requires great trust of the people, by the leaders and the people themselves. Such trust is not widespread.

CARL COHEN
The New York Times, *November 4, 1970*

He knows nothing; and he thinks he knows everything.
That points clearly to a political career.

GEORGE BERNARD SHAW
Major Barbara

The most successful politician is he who says what
everybody is thinking most often and in the loudest
voice.

THEODORE ROOSEVELT

Power is not a toy we give to good children; it is a
weapon and the strong man takes it and he uses it.

GORE VIDAL
The Best Man

There's an honest graft, and I'm an example of how it
works. I might sum up the whole thing by sayin': "I
seen my opportunities and I took 'em."

GEORGE WASHINGTON PLUNKITT

The first method for estimating the intelligence
of a ruler is to look at the men he has around him.

MACHIAVELLI
The Prince

A politician . . . one that would circumvent God.

WILLIAM SHAKESPEARE
Hamlet V:i

Politics, as the word is commonly understood, are
nothing but corruptions.

JONATHAN SWIFT
Thoughts on Various Subjects

In politics there is no honour.

BENJAMIN DISRAELI
Vivian Gray

POLITICS. The conduct of public affairs for private advantage.

AMBROSE BIERCE
The Devil's Dictionary

Politics are too serious a matter to be left to the politicians.

CHARLES DE GAULLE

I always voted at my party's call,
And I never thought of thinking for myself at all.

WILLIAM S. GILBERT
H.M.S. Pinafore

From defending the common man we pass on to exalting him. . . . Instead of demanding only that the common man may be given an opportunity to become as uncommon as possible, we make his commonness a virtue and, even in the case of candidates for high office, we sometimes praise them for being nearly indistinguishable from the average man in the street.

JOSEPH WOOD KRUTCH
Is The Common Man Too Common?

Where every man is a sharer in the direction of his ward-republic, or of some of the higher ones, and feels that he is a participator in the government of affairs, not merely at an election one day in the year, but every day; when there shall not be a man in the State who will not be a member of some one of its councils, great or small, he will let the heart be torn out of his body sooner than his power be wrested from him by a Caesar or a Bonaparte.

THOMAS JEFFERSON
Letter, February 2, 1816

X

"No Man Is an Island"

31. Friendship

No man is an island, entire of itself; every man is a
piece of the continent, a part of the main. If a clod be
washed away by the sea, Europe is the less, as well as if
a promontory were, as well as if a manor of thy friend's
or of thine own: any man's death diminishes me,
because I am involved in mankind, and therefore never
send to know for whom the bell tolls; it tolls for thee.

JOHN DONNE
Meditation XVII, Devotions upon Emergent Occasions

Behold, how good and pleasant it is for brethren to
dwell together in unity!

PSALMS 133:1

You're my friend—
What a thing friendship is, world without end!

ROBERT BROWNING
"The Flight of the Duchess"

Stranger, if you passing meet me and desire to speak
    to me,
Why should you not speak to me?
And why should I not speak to you?

WALT WHITMAN
"To You," Leaves of Grass

Let no man grumble when his friends fall off,
As they will do like leaves at the first breeze:
When your affairs come round, one way or 'tother,
Go to the coffee-house, and take another.

LORD BYRON
Don Juan

A friend is a person with whom I may be sincere.
Before him I may think aloud.

RALPH WALDO EMERSON
"Friendship," Essays

Few friendships would survive if each one knew
what his friend says of him behind his back.

BLAISE PASCAL
Pensees

Forget injuries, never forget kindnesses.

CONFUCIUS

A friend loveth at all times.

PROVERBS 17:17

He has no friend who has many friends.

ARISTOTLE
Eudemian Ethics

If a man does not make new acquaintances, as he
advances through life, he will soon find himself left
alone. A man, Sir, should keep his friendship in
constant repair.

SAMUEL JOHNSON
in Boswell's Life of Samuel Johnson, *April 7, 1755*

The only way to have a friend is to be one.
RALPH WALDO EMERSON
"Friendship," Essays

The most I can do for my friend is simply to be his friend.
HENRY DAVID THOREAU
Journal, *February 7, 1841*

He drew a circle that shut me out—
Heretic, rebel, a thing to flout.
But Love and I had the wit to win:
We drew a circle that took him in!
EDWIN MARKHAM
"Outwitted"

A friend may well be reckoned the masterpiece of Nature.
RALPH WALDO EMERSON
"Friendship," Essays

An intelligent enemy is better than a stupid friend.
AFRICAN PROVERB

Friendship is seldom lasting, but between equals, or where the superiority on one side is reduced by some equivalent advantage on the other.
SAMUEL JOHNSON
The Rambler

I was angry with my friend:
I told my wrath, my wrath did end.
I was angry with my foe:
I told it not, my wrath did grow.
WILLIAM BLAKE
"A Poison Tree," Songs of Experience

What a gamble friendship is!

E. B. WHITE
Charlotte's Web

"It isn't much fun for One, but Two
Can stick together," says Pooh, says he.
"That's how it is," says Pooh.

A. A. MILNE
"Us Two," Now We Are Six

Prosperity makes friends and adversity tries them.

PUBLILIUS SYRUS
Maxims

Should auld acquaintance be forgot,
And never brought to mind?
Should auld acquaintance be forgot,
And days of auld lang syne?

ROBERT BURNS
"Auld Lang Syne"

I haven't seen him for years. I know when we meet
there'll be no estrangement. Fondnesses retain, I'm happy
to say.

HAROLD PINTER
The New York Times, *November 18, 1971*

32. Death

The undiscover'd country, from whose bourne
No traveller returns.

WILLIAM SHAKESPEARE
Hamlet, *III:i*

There is nothing which at once affects a man so much and so little as his own death. It is a case in which the going-to-happen-ness of a thing is of greater importance than the actual thing itself.

SAMUEL BUTLER
Notebooks

Of all the wonders that I yet have heard,
It seems to me most strange that men should fear;
Seeing that death, a necessary end,
Will come when it will come.

WILLIAM SHAKESPEARE
Julius Caesar *II:2*

As he came forth of his mother's womb, naked shall he return to go as he came, and shall take nothing of his labor, which he may carry away in his hand.

ECCLESIASTES 5:15

I am convinced that it is hygienic—if I may use the word—to discover in death a goal towards which one

can strive, and that shrinking away from it is something
unhealthy and abnormal which robs the second half of
life of its purpose.

CARL G. JUNG
Psychological Reflections

"Humph," said Mary Poppins crossly, as she
plunked the toast on the table. "You can't have *anything*
for always—and don't you think it, sir!"

P. L. TRAVERS
Mary Poppins Opens the Door

When I was young I used to think that the only certain
thing about life was that I should one day die.
Now I think the only certain thing about life is that there
is no such thing as death.

SAMUEL BUTLER
Notebooks

After the first death there is no other.

DYLAN THOMAS
"A Refusal to Mourn the Death of a Child"

The fear of death is more to be dreaded than death.

PUBLILIUS SYRUS
Maxims

From too much love of living,
    From hope and fear set free,
We thank with brief thanksgiving
    Whatever gods may be
That no life lives for ever;
That dead men rise up never;
That even the weariest river
Winds somewhere safe to sea.

ALGERNON SWINBURNE
"The Garden of Proserpine"

On, on I go, (open doors of time! open hospital doors!)
The crush'd head I dress, (poor crazed hand tear not
the bandage away,)
The neck of the cavalry-man with the bullet through
and through I examine,
Hard the breathing rattles, quite glazed already the eye,
yet life struggles hard,
(Come sweet death! be persuaded oh beautiful death!
In mercy come quickly.)

WALT WHITMAN
"The Wound-Dresser," Leaves of Grass

God's finger touched him, and he slept.

ALFRED, LORD TENNYSON
"In Memoriam"

One always dies too soon—or too late. And yet one's
whole life is complete at that moment, with a line drawn
neatly under it, ready for the summing up. You are—
your life, and nothing else.

JEAN-PAUL SARTRE
No Exit

Is life a boon?
If so, it must befall,
That Death, whene'er he call,
Must call too soon.

WILLIAM S. GILBERT
The Yeomen of the Guard

Down, down, down into the darkness of the grave,
Gently they go, the beautiful, the tender, the kind;
Quietly they go, the intelligent, the witty, the brave
I know. But I do not approve. And I am not resigned.

EDNA ST. VINCENT MILLAY
"Dirge Without Music"

172

To die will be an awfully big adventure.

JAMES M. BARRIE
Peter Pan

━━━━━━━━

Because I could not stop for Death,
He kindly stopped for me;
The carriage held but just ourselves
And Immortality.

EMILY DICKINSON

━━━━━━━━

Medicine seems to be sharpening its tools to do battle with death as though death were just one more disease.

LEON R. KASS
The New York Times, *February 23, 1971*

━━━━━━━━

The process of dying is changing today. With all the new medical advances we have, we have to determine if life is really being served by prolonging the act of dying.

DONALD W. MC KINNEY
The New York Times, *March 1, 1971*

━━━━━━━━

Everyone who loves is vulnerable to the pain of grief, for love means attachment and all human attachments are subject to loss. But grief need not, should not, be a destructive emotion.

JOYCE BROTHERS
Good Housekeeping, *January 1971*

33. What Is Man?

At the beginning, you were no bigger than a dot, much smaller even than the dot on this page, or a single grain of sand. You were like a tiny little round egg, so small that it could not be seen at all, except through a microscope.

You began from a tiny egg cell in your mother's body called an *ovum*, joined with something else—even tinier —from your father's body. This something else was a special kind of cell called a sperm.

SIDONIE MATSNER GRUENBERG
The Wonderful Story of How You Were Born

Men at some time are masters of their fates;
The fault, dear Brutus, is not in our stars,
But in ourselves, that we are underlings.

WILLIAM SHAKESPEARE
Julius Caesar, *I:iii*

Man is the only animal for whom his own experience is a problem which he has to solve and from which he cannot escape.

ERICH FROMM
Man For Himself

What a piece of work is man! How noble in reason! How infinite in faculty! In form and moving how express and admirable! In action how like an angel! In apprehension how like a god! The beauty of the world, the paragon of animals.

WILLIAM SHAKESPEARE
Hamlet, II:ii

We are as gods and might as well get good at it.

WHOLE EARTH CATALOG
Fall 1969

Do I contradict myself? Very well, I contradict myself. I am large, and I contain multitudes.

WALT WHITMAN
Leaves of Grass

The most luxurious possession, the richest treasure anybody has, is his personal dignity.

JACKIE ROBINSON
I Never Had It Made

Man is the only animal whose desires increase as they are fed; the only animal that is never satisfied.

HENRY GEORGE

The tragedy of man is that he can conceive self-perfection but cannot achieve it.

REINHOLD NIEBUHR
The New York Times, June 2, 1971

Man is an enigma; indivisible and yet complex; he is composed of hundreds of separate parts that are constantly dying and being renewed, yet he retains a mysterious "individuality." The human being may be compared to a cooperative society whose members band together for mutual support and protection, presenting a common front to the external world, and sharing equally in the privileges and responsibilities of their internal world.

MARGARET SHEA GILBERT
"Biography of the Unborn"

Give a chimpanzee a few chimpanzees, a peaceful stretch of jungle and plenty of bananas, and it will live happily for the rest of its life. Give a man an environment correspondingly idyllic, say a Garden of Eden, and he will get into trouble. Getting into trouble is our genius and glory as a species.

JOHN PFEIFFER
"Introducing the Brain"

An ordinary human being is a lump of matter weighing between 50 and 100 kilograms. This living matter is the same matter of which the rest of the earth, the sun, and even the most distant stars and nebulae are made.

JULIAN HUXLEY
"Variations on a Theme by Darwin"

How many and deep are the divisions between human beings! Not only are there divisions between races, nations, classes and religions, but also an almost total incomprehension between the sexes, the old and the young, the sick and the healthy. There would be no society if living together depended upon understanding each other.

ERIC HOFFER
The New York Times Magazine, April 25, 1971

The worst sin towards our fellow creatures is not to hate them, but to be indifferent to them; that's the essence of inhumanity.

GEORGE BERNARD SHAW
The Devil's Disciple

Language was invented to ask questions. Answers may be given by grunts and gestures, but questions must be spoken. Humanness came of age when man asked the first question. Social stagnation results not from lack of answers but from the absence of the impulse to ask questions.

ERIC HOFFER
The New York Times Magazine, *April 25, 1971*

For the first time in all time, a living creature understands its origin and can undertake to design its future.

ROBERT SINSHEIMER
Time, *April 19, 1971*

I believe man will not merely endure, he will prevail. He is immortal, not because he, alone among creatures, has an inexhaustible voice but because he has a soul, a spirit, capable of compassion and sacrifice and endurance. The poet's, the writer's duty is to write about these things.

WILLIAM FAULKNER
Nobel Prize Acceptance Speech, 1950

The first cry of a newborn baby in Chicago or Zamboango, in Amsterdam or Rangoon, has the same pitch and key, each saying, "I am! I have come through! I belong! I am a member of the Family."

CARL SANDBURG
Museum of Modern Art
Prologue to exhibit
Family of Man (*1955*)

There is only one man in the world
and his name is All Men.
There is only one woman in the world
and her name is All Women.

There is only one child in the world
and the child's name is All Children.
                                CARL SANDBURG
                            Museum of Modern Art
                            Prologue to exhibit
                            Family of Man (*1955*)

========

Man is a unique animal insofar as he is able to identify
with the feelings of others. He needs to feel a sense of
community, to identify himself as a member of a society
in which he is not a bystander.
                            SEYMOUR L. HALLECK
              "Why They'd Rather Do Their Own Thing,"
                            Think *Magazine 1968*

========

Man is simply the most formidable of all the beasts
of prey, and, indeed, the only one that preys
systematically on its own species.
                                WILLIAM JAMES
                        Address, October 7, 1904

========

The human baby does not have his future way of life
spelled out for him by instincts. Only after he is born
can he learn the customs by which his society expects
him to live. But he can be taught these customs so well
that in time they will seem as natural to him as it is for
an ant to live as an ant and not as a bee or a grasshopper.
In a way, therefore, human beings are made, not born.
Man makes himself. That is why there can be so many
different ways of being human.
                                GENE LISITZKY
                        Four Ways of Being Human

========

There are one hundred and ninety-three living species
of monkeys and apes. One hundred and ninety-two of
them are covered with hair. The exception is a naked
ape self-named *Homo sapiens*.
                                DESMOND MORRIS
                                The Naked Ape

What is essential in the existence of man is the fact that he has emerged from the animal kingdom . . . that he has transcended nature—although he never leaves it; he is a part of it. . . . Man can only go forward by developing his reason, by finding a new harmony, a human one, instead of the prehuman harmony which is irretrievably lost.

ERICH FROMM
The Art of Loving

The belief in a supernatural source of evil is not necessary; men alone are quite capable of every wickedness.

JOSEPH CONRAD
Under Western Eyes

The more you see of people here or anywhere else, the more you realize that the whole world's like a play. You can change the costumes and some of the lines, but the characters are the same all over.

LUELLA FOSTER
Peace Corps volunteer in Niger,
The New York Times, *November 30, 1970*

Evil is unspectacular and always human
And shares our bed and eats at our own table.

W. H. AUDEN
"Herman Melville"

The anthropologist, as he pondered his growing body of material upon the customs of primitive people, grew to realize the tremendous role played in an individual's life by the social environment in which each is born and reared. One by one, aspects of behavior which we had been accustomed to consider invariable complements of our humanity were found to be merely a result of civilization present in the inhabitants of one country, absent in another country, and this without a change of race.

MARGARET MEAD
From the South Seas

———————

One of the most widespread superstitions is that every man has his own special, definite qualities: That a man is kind, cruel, wise, stupid, energetic, apathetic, etc. Men are not like that . . . men are like rivers . . . every river narrows here, is more rapid there, here slower, there broader, now clear, now cold, now dull, now warm. It is the same with men. Every man carries in himself the germs of every human quality, and sometimes one manifests itself, sometimes another, and the man often becomes unlike himself, while still remaining the same man.

LEO TOLSTOY

XI

"Earth's the Right Place for Love"

34. Love

Earth's the right place for love:
I don't know where it's likely to go better.

ROBERT FROST
"Birches"

Love cannot endure indifference. It needs to be wanted.
Like a lamp, it needs to be fed out of the oil of another's
heart, or its flame burns low.

HENRY WARD BEECHER

My love is like a red red rose
    That's newly spung in June:
My love is like the melodie
    That's sweetly play'd in tune.

ROBERT BURNS
"My Love Is Like a Red Red Rose"

Love is a medicine for the sickness of the world; a
prescription often given, too rarely taken.

KARL MENNINGER

If I truly love one person I love all persons, I love the
world, I love life. If I can say to somebody else, "I love
you," I must be able to say, "I love in you everybody, I
love through you the world, I love in you also myself."

ERICH FROMM
The Art of Loving

It is easier to love humanity as a whole than to love one's neighbor.

ERIC HOFFER

Thou shalt love thy neighbour as thyself.

MATTHEW 19:19

We love the things we love for what they are.

ROBERT FROST
"Hyla Brook"

One does not *fall* into love; one *grows* into love, and love grows in him.

KARL MENNINGER

The pleasure of love is in loving. We are happier in the passion we feel than in that we inspire.

FRANCOIS LA ROCHEFOUCAULD
Reflections

Infantile love follows the principle: "I love because I am loved." Mature love follows the principle: "I am loved because I love." Immature love says: "I love you because I need you." Mature love says: "I need you because I love you."

ERICH FROMM
The Art of Loving

Sigh no more, ladies, sigh no more,
Men were deceivers ever,
One foot in sea and one on shore;
To one thing constant never.

WILLIAM SHAKESPEARE
Much Ado About Nothing, *II:iii*

Does the imagination dwell the most
Upon a woman won or a woman lost?

WILLIAM BUTLER YEATS
"The Tower"

Love begets love.

ROBERT HERRICK
Hesperides

Many waters cannot quench love, neither can the
floods drown it.

SONG OF SOLOMON 8:7

My bounty is as boundless as the sea,
My love as deep; the more I give to thee
The more I have, for both are infinite.

WILLIAM SHAKESPEARE
Romeo and Juliet, II:ii

Oh, love is warm when it is new,
And love is sweet when it is true;
But love grows old and waxeth cold,
And fades away like morning dew.

AMERICAN FOLK SONG
"The Water Is Wide"

Will you love me in December as you do in May
Will you love me in the good old fashioned way?
When my hair has all turned gray.
Will you kiss me then and say,
That you love me in December as you do in May?

JAMES J. WALKER
"Will You Love Me in December?"

All love is sweet,
Given or returned. Common as light is love,
And its familiar voice wearies not ever.

PERCY BYSSHE SHELLEY
Promethius Unbound

Love, love, tender love,
Where are you tonight?
Moon and stars shine from above,
But without you, there is no light.

Love, love, tender love,
Hear my lonely cry.
Moon and stars die up above,
And without you, then so will I.

AMERICAN FOLK SONG
"Tender Love"

Oh, when I was in love with you,
Then I was clean and brave,
And miles around the wonder grew
How well did I behave.

And now the fancy passes by,
And nothing will remain,
And miles around they'll say that I
Am quite myself again.

A. E. HOUSMAN
A Shropshire Lad

You've got to love what's lovable and hate what's
hateable. It takes brains to see the difference.

ROBERT FROST

And the wish to kill is never killed, but with some gift
of courage one may look into its face when it appears,

and with a stroke of love—as to an idiot in the house—
forgive it; again and again . . . forever?

ARTHUR MILLER
After the Fall

35. Hate

Hatred comes from the heart; contempt from the head;
and neither feeling is quite within our control.

ARTHUR SCHOPENHAUER
Studies in Pessimism

Hatred is a settled anger.

CICERO
The Tusculan Disputations

Hell is—other people!

JEAN-PAUL SARTRE
No Exit

A man cannot be too careful in the choice of his
enemies.

OSCAR WILDE
The Picture of Dorian Gray

The most important evils that mankind have to
consider are those which they inflict upon each other
through stupidity or malevolence or both.

BERTRAND RUSSELL
"Ideas That Have Harmed Mankind," Unpopular Essays

Fear gone, there can be no hatred.

MOHANDAS K. GANDHI

Hate is a dead thing. Who of us would be a tomb?

KAHLIL GIBRAN

When angry, count ten before you speak; if very
angry, an hundred.

THOMAS JEFFERSON
A Decalogue of Canons of Observation in Practical Life

If you have no enemies, it is a sign fortune has forgot
you.

THOMAS FULLER
Gnomologia

It does not matter much what a man hates providing
he hates something.

SAMUEL BUTLER
Notebooks

Love, friendship, respect, do not unite people as much
as a common hatred for something.

ANTON CHEKHOV
Notebooks

It is a human nature to hate those whom we have
injured.

TACITUS
Agricola

The hatred of relatives is the most violent.

TACITUS
Annals

A face devoid of love or grace,
A hateful, hard, successful face,
A face with which a stone
Would feel as thoroughly at ease
As were they old acquaintances—
First time together thrown.

EMILY DICKINSON

---

36. Other Feelings

If a man can cry, then he has feelings. Indians cry all
the time. We get together and sing songs, and we cry
in these songs. But this society is very machine-like, and
so we begin to act like machines and then we become
machines.

WILFRED PELLETIER
The New York Times, *March 3, 1971*

What I was really hanging around for, I was trying
to feel some kind of a good-by. I mean I've left schools
and places and I didn't even know I was leaving them.
I hate that. I don't care if it's a sad good-by or a bad
good-by, but when I leave a place I like to *know* I'm
leaving it. If you don't, you feel even worse.

J. D. SALINGER
The Catcher in the Rye

I can generally bear the separation, but I don't like
the leave-taking.

SAMUEL BUTLER
Notebooks

Why can't we get all the people together in the world that we really like and then just stay together? I guess that wouldn't work. Someone would leave. Someone always leaves and then we have to say good-bye. I hate good-byes. I know what I need. I need more hellos.

SNOOPY
in comic strip Peanuts
by Charles M. Schulz

This is my last message to you: in sorrow seek happiness.

FEODOR DOSTOYEVSKY
The Brothers Karamazov

It is good to grow wise by sorrow.

AESCHYLUS
Eumenides

"After so many years he still keeps finding
Good arguments he sees he might have used.
I sympathize. I know just how it feels
To think of the right thing to say too late."

ROBERT FROST
"The Death of The Hired Man"

I remember once back about five years ago . . . I said the right thing.

CHARLIE BROWN
in comic strip Peanuts
by Charles M. Schulz

He who feels no compassion will become insane.

HASIDIC SAYING

One cannot live with sighted eyes and feeling heart
and not know and react to the miseries which afflict
this world.

LORRAINE HANSBERRY
in To Be Young, Gifted and Black

To the little child is given the keep of happiness, and
the key, likewise of wisdom. He trails his fingers in cool
water, and it is enough to make him laugh and sing
with the gladness of living. He breathes the spring wind,
or watches snowflakes falling, or stares at the patterned
lichen on a stone, and his heart is set singing with the
glory and the wonder of the world.

ALAN DEVOE
Down to Earth

How is it that Daddy was never any support to me in
my struggle, why did he completely miss the mark when
he wanted to offer me a helping hand? Daddy tried the
wrong methods, he always talked to me as a child who
was going through difficult phases. It sounds crazy,
because Daddy's the only one who has always taken me
into his confidence and no one but Daddy has given me
the feeling that I'm sensible. But there's one thing he's
omitted: you see, he hasn't realized that for me the fight
to get on top was more important than all else. I didn't
want to hear about "symptoms of your age," or "other
girls," or "it wears off by itself"; I didn't want to be
treated as a girl-like-all-others, but as Anne on her own
merits.

ANNE FRANK
The Diary of a Young Girl

The thought of death made Stuart sad, and he began
to think of his home and of his father and mother and
brother and of Margalo and Snowbell . . . and of what
a pleasant place his home was, specially in the early

morning with the light just coming in through the curtains
and the household stirring and waking.

E. B. WHITE
Stuart Little

———————

The artist is only given to sense more keenly than
others the harmony of the world and all the beauty and
savagery of the human contribution to it—and to
communicate this poignantly to people.

ALEKSANDR I. SOLZHENITSYN
Nobel Prize Acceptance Speech, 1972

XII

"Facing It—
Always Facing It"

37. Responsibility

Facing it—always facing it—that's the way to get through. Face it! That's enough for any man.

JOSEPH CONRAD

Life is to be lived; there is no help for it.

ELEANOR ROOSEVELT
in Eleanor: The Years Alone
by Joseph P. Lash

The idea that a State, any more than a corporation, commits crimes is a fiction. Crimes always are committed only by persons.

ROBERT H. JACKSON
comments at start of Nuremberg war crimes trials,
November 1945

Whosoever saves a single life is as if he had saved the whole world; whosoever destroys a single life is as if he had destroyed the whole world.

THE TALMUD

Be not afraid of greatness: some men are born great, some achieve greatness, and some have greatness thrust upon them.

WILLIAM SHAKESPEARE
Twelfth Night, *II:v*

Life is not an exact science, it is an art.

SAMUEL BUTLER
Notebooks

The woods are lovely, dark, and deep.
But I have promises to keep,
And miles to go before I sleep,
And miles to go before I sleep.

ROBERT FROST
"*Stopping by Woods on a Snowy Evening*"

Do not free a camel of the burden of his hump. You
may be freeing him from being a camel.

G. K. CHESTERTON

Never trouble another for what you can do yourself.

THOMAS JEFFERSON
Letter, February 21, 1825

Make it a point to do something every day that you
don't want to do. This is the golden rule for acquiring
the habit of doing your duty without pain.

MARK TWAIN

Life only demands from you the strength you possess.
Only one feat is possible—not to have run away.

DAG HAMMARSKJÖLD

The sea rises, the light fails, lovers cling to each other,
and children cling to us. The moment we cease to
hold each other, the moment we break faith with one
another, the sea engulfs us and the light goes out.

JAMES BALDWIN

It seemed to me a matter of course that we should all
take our share of the burden of pain which lies upon
the world.

ALBERT SCHWEITZER

If I am not for myself, who will be for me? If I am not
for others, who am I for? And if not now, when?

THE TALMUD

For, assuredly, nobody will care for him who
cares for nobody.

THOMAS JEFFERSON
Letter, October 12, 1786

If you are given three wishes, you must be very careful
what you wish for.

NORBERT WIENER

With surpassing ease and a cool sense of authority, the
children of plenty have voiced an intention to live by a
different ethical standard than their parents
accepted. The pleasure principle has been elevated over
the Puritan ethic of work. To do one's own thing is a
greater duty than to be a useful citizen. Personal freedom
in the midst of squalor is more liberating than social
conformity with the trappings of wealth. Now that youth
takes abundance for granted, it can afford to reject
materialism.

"Essay," Time, *August 29, 1969*

There are various routes of escape from responsibility:
escape into death, escape into disease, and escape into
stupidity. The last is the safest and easiest, for even
intelligent people are usually closer to the goal than they
would like to think.

ARTHUR SCHNITZLER

The hippies have shown that it can be pleasant to
drop out of the arduous task of attempting to steer a
difficult unrewarding society. But when that is done,
you leave the driving to the Hell's Angels.

WARREN HINCKLE
"A Social History of The Hippies," Ramparts, 1967

The individual has no recourse from the necessity
of making final decisions for himself, and to make
them in the last analysis in freedom and isolation may
require literally as well as figuratively an agony
of anxiety and inward struggle.

ROLLO MAY
The New York Times Magazine, March 28, 1971

38. Fear and Uncertainty

You gain strength, courage and confidence by
every experience in which you really stop to look
fear in the face. You are able to say to yourself, "I have
lived through this horror. I can take the next thing
that comes along." . . . You must do the thing you
think you cannot do.

ELEANOR ROOSEVELT

Life must go on,
And the dead be forgotten;
Life must go on,
Though good men die;
Anne, eat your breakfast;

Dan, take your medicine;
Life must go on;
I forget just why.

EDNA ST. VINCENT MILLAY
"Lament"

Men die of fright and live of confidence.

HENRY DAVID THOREAU

There are two ways of avoiding fear: one is by
persuading ourselves that we are immune from disaster,
and the other is by the practice of sheer courage.
The latter is difficult, and to everybody becomes
impossible at a certain point. The former has therefore
always been more popular.

BERTRAND RUSSELL
"An Outline of Intellectual Rubbish," Unpopular Essays

I will show you fear in a handful of dust.

T. S. ELIOT
The Waste Land

Thou shalt not be afraid for the terror by night;
nor the arrow that flieth by day.

PSALMS 91:5

. . . rather bear those ills
we have
Than fly to others that we know not of.

WILLIAM SHAKESPEARE
Hamlet, III:2

Ah, love, let us be true
To one another! for the world, which seems

To lie before us like a land of dreams,
So various, so beautiful, so new,
Hath really neither joy, nor love, nor light,
Not certitude, nor peace, nor help for pain;
And we are here, as on a darkling plain
Swept with confused alarms of struggle and flight,
Where ignorant armies clash by night.

MATTHEW ARNOLD
"Dover Beach"

He has no hope who never had a fear.

WILLIAM COWPER
Truth

He who fears he will suffer, already suffers
because of his fear.

MONTAIGNE
"Fear," Essays

Like one, that on a lonesome road
　　Doth walk in fear and dread,
And having once turned round walks on,
　　And turns no more his head;
Because he knows a frightful fiend
　　Doth close behind him tread.

SAMUEL TAYLOR COLERIDGE
"The Rime of The Ancient Mariner"

Humans always have fear of an unknown situation—
this is normal. The important thing is what we do
about it. If fear is permitted to become a paralyzing
thing that interferes with proper action, then it is
harmful. The best antidote to fear is to know all we
can about a situation.

JOHN H. GLENN, JR.

But now, I am cabin'd, cribb'd, confin'd, bound in
To saucy doubts and fears.

WILLIAM SHAKESPEARE
Macbeth, III:4

Fear is one of the possessions of human nature
of which it is impossible to divest it. You
remember the Emperor Charles V, when he read upon
the tombstone of a Spanish nobleman, "Here lies
one who never knew fear," wittily said, "Then
he never snuffed a candle with his fingers."

SAMUEL JOHNSON

Defect of judgment
Is oft the cure of fear.

WILLIAM SHAKESPEARE
Cymbeline, IV:2

He must necessarily fear many, whom many fear.

SENECA
"De Ira"

The thing in the world I am most afraid of is fear, and
with good reason; that passion alone, in the trouble of it,
exceeding all other accidents.

MONTAIGNE
"Fear," Essays

The only thing we have to fear is fear itself—nameless,
unreasoning, unjustified terror which paralyzes
needed efforts to convert retreat into advance.

FRANKLIN D. ROOSEVELT
First Inaugural Address, March 4, 1933

39. Solitude and Loneliness

Youth has been lonely for centuries. What has "alienation" got that differentiates it from old-fashioned loneliness?

SPENCER BROWN
"We Can't Appease the Younger Generation,"
The New York Times Magazine, *November 27, 1966*

Only when you have worked alone—when you have felt around you a black gulf of solitude more isolating than that which surrounds the dying man, and in hope and in despair have trusted to your own unshaken will—then only will you have achieved.

OLIVER WENDELL HOLMES
The Mind and Faith of Justice Holmes

To be alone is the fate of all great minds— a fate deplored at times, but still always chosen as the less grievous of two evils.

ARTHUR SCHOPENHAUER
Our Relation to Ourselves

The happiest of all lives is a busy solitude.

VOLTAIRE
Letter to Frederick the Great, *1751*

He is never less at leisure than when at leisure, nor
less alone than when he is alone.

CICERO
De Officiis

Loneliness . . . is and always has been the central
and inevitable experience of every man.

THOMAS WOLFE
You Can't Go Home Again

The deepest need of man, then, is the need
to overcome his separateness, to leave the
prison of his aloneness.

ERICH FROMM
The Art of Loving

How lonely we are in the world! . . . Ah, sir, a distinct
universe walks about under your hat and under mine,—
all things in nature are different to each,—the woman we
look at has not the same features, the dish we eat
from has not the same taste to one and the other,—
you and I are but a pair of infinite isolations, with
some fellow-islands a little more or less near to us.

WILLIAM MAKEPEACE THACKERAY
Pendennis

Alone, alone—all, all alone,
Alone on a wide, wide sea.

SAMUEL TAYLOR COLERIDGE
"The Rime of The Ancient Mariner"

Ain't it hard to stumble
When you got no place to fall?
Ain't it hard to stumble
When you got no place to fall?

202

In this whole wide world,
I got no place at all.
I'm a stranger here, a stranger everywhere,
I could go home, but honey, I'm a stranger there.

BLACK AMERICAN BLUES
"I'm a Stranger Here"

I have a house where I go
    When there's too many people,
I have a house where I go
    Where no one can be;
I have a house where I go,
Where nobody ever says "No";
Where no one says anything—so
There is no one but me.

A. A. MILNE
"Solitude," Now We Are Six

"I fly from pleasure," said the prince, "because
pleasure has ceased to please; I am lonely because
I am miserable, and am unwilling to cloud with my
presence the happiness of others."

SAMUEL JOHNSON
Rasselas

I never found the companion that was so
companionable as solitude.

HENRY DAVID THOREAU
"Solitude," Walden

My heart is a lonely hunter that hunts on a lonely hill.

WILLIAM SHARP (FIONA MACLEOD)
"The Lonely Hunter"

XIII

"The Voyage of Their Life"

40. Experience and Action

There is a tide in the affairs of men,
Which, taken at the flood, leads on to fortune;
Omitted, all the voyage of their life
Is bound in shallows and in miseries.

WILLIAM SHAKESPEARE
Julius Caesar, *IV:iii*

It is for you to know all; it is for you to dare all.

RALPH WALDO EMERSON

This little light of mine,
I'm gonna let it shine.
This little light of mine,
I'm gonna let it shine.
This little light of mine,
I'm gonna let it shine,
Ev'ry day, ev'ry way,
Ev'ry day, ev'ry way,
Gonna let my little light shine.

GOSPEL SONG
"This Little Light of Mine"

The mark of the immature man is that he wants to
die nobly for a cause, while the mark of the mature
man is that he wants to live humbly for one.

WILHELM STEKEL

Live dangerously and you live right.

JOHANN VON GOETHE
Faust

---

an optimist is a guy
that has never had
much experience

DON MARQUIS
"certain maxims of archy," Archy and Mehitabel

Live all you can; it's a mistake not to.

HENRY JAMES
The Ambassadors

Don't sidle in as if you were doubtful
Whether you're welcome—the feast is yours!
Nor take but a little, refusing more
With a bashful "Thank you," when you're hungry.
Is your soul alive? Then let it feed!

. . .

You will die, no doubt, but die while living
In depths of azure, rapt and mated,
Kissing the queen-bee, Life!

EDGAR LEE MASTERS
"Edmund Pollard," Spoon River Anthology

For of all sad words of tongue or pen,
The saddest are these: "It might have been!"

JOHN GREENLEAF WHITTIER
"Maud Muller"

No, you never get any fun
Out of the things you haven't done.

OGDEN NASH
"Portrait of the Artist as a Prematurely Old Man"

If a lion eats me, you will hear the news from him.
He will say, "The old man was tough, but a tasty meal."

IGOR STRAVINSKY
before going to Africa on a conducting tour,
quoted in obituary, Time, *April 19, 1971*

I am never bored. Everybody is much more
interesting than myself, whom I know already.

LILI KRAUS
The New York Times, *April 6, 1971*

The elders are a strangely isolated generation. No
other generation has ever known, experienced, and
struggled to incorporate such massive and rapid
change—has watched while the sources of energy, the
means of communication, the certainties of a known
world, the limits of the explorable universe, the definition
of humanity, and the fundamental imperatives of life
and death have changed before their eyes. Adults today
know more about change than any previous generation.

MARGARET MEAD
Culture and Commitment

Everyone whose deeds are more than his wisdom, his
wisdom endures. And everyone whose wisdom is
more than his deeds his wisdom does not endure.

THE TALMUD

To most men, experience is like the stern lights of a
ship, which illumine only the track it has passed.

SAMUEL TAYLOR COLERIDGE
Table-Talk

Doubt, of whatever kind, can be ended by
Action alone.

THOMAS CARLYLE
Past and Present

QUENTIN: You know? There's one word written on
  your forehead.
MAGGIE: What?
QUENTIN: "Now."
MAGGIE: But what else is there?

ARTHUR MILLER
After the Fall

We saw the risk we took in doing good,
But dared not spare to do the best we could
Though harm should come of it.

ROBERT FROST
"The Exposed Nest"

Life is action and passion; therefore, it is required
of a man that he should share the passion and action
of his time at peril of being judged not to have lived.

OLIVER WENDELL HOLMES

Believe not your own brother—believe instead your
own crooked eye.

RUSSIAN PROVERB
quoted by Aleksandr I. Solzhenitsyn in
Nobel Prize Acceptance Speech, 1972

There are no elders who know what those who have
been reared within the last twenty years know about the
world into which they were born.

MARGARET MEAD
Culture and Commitment

Nobody can become perfect by merely ceasing to act.

BHAGAVAD-GITA

We learn from experience that men never learn
anything from experience.

GEORGE BERNARD SHAW

Living is a constant process of deciding what
we are going to do.

JOSÉ ORTEGA Y GASSET

Two roads diverged in a wood, and I—
I took the one less traveled by,
And that has made all the difference.

ROBERT FROST
"The Road Not Taken"

I never liked the middle ground—the most
boring place in the world.

LOUISE NEVELSON
The New York Times Magazine, *January 24, 1971*

If you cannot catch the bird of paradise better
take a wet hen.

NIKITA KHRUSHCHEV

Somewhere along the line of development we discover
what we really are, and then we make our real
decision for which we are responsible. Make that
decision primarily for yourself because you can
never live anyone else's life, not even your
child's. The influence you exert is through your
own life and what you become yourself.

ELEANOR ROOSEVELT
Letter, June 1941

The art of living is more like that of wrestling
than of dancing; the main thing is to stand firm
and be ready for an unforeseen attack.

MARCUS AURELIUS

It is when we all play safe that we create a world
of the utmost insecurity.

DAG HAMMARSKJÖLD

The last temptation is the greatest treason:
To do the right deed for the wrong reason.

T. S. ELIOT
Murder in the Cathedral

Your way of giving is more important than
what you give.

VIETNAMESE PROVERB

The past is a foreign country: they do
things differently there.

L. P. HARTLEY
The Go-Between

To exclude from positions of trust and command
all those below the age of 44 would have kept
Jefferson from writing the Declaration of Independence,
Washington from commanding the Continental Army,
Madison from fathering the Constitution, Hamilton
from serving as Secretary of the Treasury, Clay from
being elected Speaker of the House, and
Christopher Columbus from discovering America.

JOHN F. KENNEDY
The New York Times, July 5, 1960

Give God Time.

THE KORAN

41. The Search for Truth

A nice old lady, well-bred and what is called
well-educated, once remarked to me in passing that the
giant waterbugs one often sees flying about street
lights in southern cities were generated by the electric
current, and when I expressed some skepticism
concerning this novel theory of the origin of life she
was ready with a proof. They had never been seen
in her town until electricity was brought there.

> JOSEPH WOOD KRUTCH
> The Desert Year

The world begins to exist when the individual
discovers it.

> CARL G. JUNG
> Psychological Reflections

The office of the scholar is to cheer, to raise, and to
guide men by showing them facts amidst appearances.

> RALPH WALDO EMERSON
> The American Scholar

There is one outstandingly important fact regarding
spaceship Earth, and that is that no instruction book
came with it. . . . Because of the lack of an instruction
book, we were forced to use our intellect, which is our
supreme faculty, to devise scientific experimental
procedures and to effectively interpret the significance
of the experimental findings.

> R. BUCKMINSTER FULLER
> Our Spaceship Earth

Knowledge, in truth, is the great sun in the firmament.
Life and power are scattered with all its beams.

DANIEL WEBSTER
Address, 1825

Discovery consists of seeing what everybody has
seen and thinking what nobody has thought.

ALBERT SZENT-GYÖRGYI

Thinking is the talking of the soul with itself.

PLATO

There are no whole truths: all truths are half truths.

ALFRED NORTH WHITEHEAD
Dialogues

For he who'd make his fellow-creatures wise
Should always gild the philosophic pill.

WILLIAM S. GILBERT
The Yeomen of The Guard

God offers to every mind its choice between truth
and repose. Take which you please—
you can never have both.

RALPH WALDO EMERSON
"Intellect"

Canst thou by searching find out God?

JOB 11:7

If a man will begin with certainties, he shall
end in doubts; but if he will be content to begin
with doubts, he shall end in certainties.

FRANCIS BACON
"Advancement of Learning"

Thinking you know when in fact you don't is a fatal
mistake, to which we are all prone.

BERTRAND RUSSELL
"An Outline of Intellectual Rubbish," Unpopular Essays

Don't you see? I'm not young enough
to know everything.

JAMES M. BARRIE
The Admirable Crichton

Every one should keep a mental waste-paper basket
and the older he grows the more things he will consign to
it—torn up to irrevocable tatters.

SAMUEL BUTLER
Notebooks

Even in the deepest sinking there is the hidden
purpose of an ultimate rising. Thus it is for all men:
from none is the source of life withheld unless he
himself withdraws from it. Therefore the most
important thing is not to despair.

HASIDIC SAYING

There is no love of life without despair of life.

ALBERT CAMUS
A Happy Death

He who receives an idea from me, receives instruction
himself without lessening mine; as he who lights his
taper at mine, receives light without darkening me.

THOMAS JEFFERSON
Letter, August 13, 1813

The one and only substitute for experience which we
have not ourselves had is art, literature. We have been

given a miraculous faculty: Despite the differences of language, customs and social structure we are able to communicate life experience from one whole nation to another, to communicate a difficult national experience many decades long which the second of the two has never experienced.

ALEKSANDR I. SOLZHENITSYN
Nobel Prize Acceptance Speech, 1972

Say not, "I have found the truth," but rather, "I have found a truth."

KAHLIL GIBRAN
The Prophet

This business of being sincere in life and to life is a vital one. It is really the most vital one in the world. If you have sincerity, all other things will be added to you. Everyone realizes the value of sincerity in, say, acting. We expect sincerity from our politicians (such is the optimism of mankind), from our judges and magistrates, teachers and doctors. Yet we educate our children in such a way that they dare not be sincere.

A. S. NEILL
Summerhill: A Radical Approach to Child Rearing

How are you going to see the sun if you lie on your stomach?

ASHANTI PROVERB

42. Education

All of us have two educations: one which we
receive from others; another, and the
most valuable, which we give ourselves.

JOHN RANDOLPH

Education, beyond all other devices of human
origin, is the great equalizer of the conditions
of men—the balance-wheel of the social
machinery. . . . It does better than to disarm the poor
of their hostility towards the rich; it prevents being poor.

HORACE MANN

If Erasmus saw the classroom as the new stage for
the drama of the printing press, we can see today
that the new situation for young and old alike is the
classroom without walls. The entire urban
environment has become aggressively pedagogic.
Everybody and everything has a message to declare,
a line to plug.

MARSHALL MC LUHAN
Sight, Sound and Fury

Conversation is the laboratory and workshop of
the student.

RALPH WALDO EMERSON

Now the purpose of education—I mean real
education—is to set up a current of understanding
between the student and the things of the world
in which he lives. In the process of learning the student
begins to look at things in books. . . . The only purpose
of his study is to get the life current of understanding
started. Once it begins to flicker, he reads more books
as his intellectual curiosity drives him on. It is when
he is able to lay the book down and examine the rock or
the star or the blade of grass for himself and with
understanding that he begins to be educated. . . . Once
educated, he turns to things not found in
universities, but at large.

WALTER PRESCOTT WEBB
An Honest Preface

___

The pupil who is never required to do what he
cannot do, never does what he can do.

JOHN STUART MILL

___

Children would not be sent [to schools] by their
parents at all if they did not act as prisons in which
the immature are kept from worrying the mature.

GEORGE BERNARD SHAW
Preface, Back to Methuselah

___

School days, I believe, are the unhappiest in the
whole span of human existence. They are full of dull,
unintelligible tasks, new and unpleasant ordinances,
brutal violations of common sense and common decency.
It doesn't take a reasonably bright boy long to discover
that most of what is rammed into him is nonsense,
and that no one really cares very much whether
he learns it or not.

H. L. MENCKEN
The Vintage Mencken

Chance favors the prepared mind.

LOUIS PASTEUR

Teaching is not a lost art, but the regard for it
is a lost tradition.

JACQUES BARZUN
Newsweek, December 5, 1955

"Do you think you can maintain discipline?" asked
the Superintendent.
"Of course I can," replied Stuart. "I'll make the work
interesting and the discipline will take care of itself."

E. B. WHITE
Stuart Little

What will have to happen before those who teach learn
a new tone of voice so that those who are taught
can hear what they say?

MARGARET MEAD
New Lives for Old

Somehow the notion has got abroad that education is
confined to reservations as were the Indians. . . . The
biggest reservations are called universities and it is
too generally assumed that they have a sort of monopoly
on knowledge and the facilities for acquiring it.
What they really have is a vast number of descriptions
which are called books and a somewhat lesser number
of describers called teachers. We can never have
real education, or a self-perpetuating culture, until we
get beyond the description and the describer to the
things described. In short, education needs to be
got off the reservations. . . .

WALTER PRESCOTT WEBB
An Honest Preface

Too much schooling works against education.

JOHN HOLT
Freedom and Beyond

To learn is to change. Education is a process that
changes the learner.

GEORGE B. LEONARD
Education and Ecstasy

Learning learns but one lesson: doubt!

GEORGE BERNARD SHAW
The Admirable Bashville

I have never let my schooling interfere with my
education.

MARK TWAIN

No man can be a pure specialist without being in the
strict sense an idiot.

GEORGE BERNARD SHAW
Maxims for Revolutionists

Then to unlearn the first ideas of history, of science,
of social institutions, to unlearn one's own life and
purpose; to unlearn the old mode of thought and way
of arriving at things; to take off peel after peel, and so
get by degrees slowly towards the truth—thus writing as
it were, a sort of floating book in the mind, almost
remaking the soul. It seems as if the chief value of books
is to give us something to unlearn.

RICHARD JEFFRIES

I have often reflected upon the new vistas that
reading opened to me. I knew right there in prison that

reading had changed forever the course of my life. As I see it today, the ability to read awoke inside me some long dormant craving to be mentally alive.

MALCOLM X
Autobiography

... People in school today can expect a lifetime in which knowledge itself will radically change—not only in its details but its structures; so that the mark of a truly educated man will no longer be how much or even how variously he now knows, but how quickly and how completely he can continually learn.

RICHARD KOSTELANETZ
Introduction, Human Alternatives: Visions for Us Now

There is no great concurrence between learning and wisdom.

FRANCIS BACON
"Civil Knowledge"

The educated man is a greater nuisance than the uneducated one.

GEORGE BERNARD SHAW
Preface, Back to Methuselah

XIV

"Every Question... Leads on to Another"

43. Science

With us, the infantile inquisitiveness is strengthened
and stretched out into our mature years. We never
stop investigating. We are never satisfied that we know
enough to get by. Every question we answer leads on
to another question. This has become the greatest
survival trick of our species.

DESMOND MORRIS
The Naked Ape

The most incomprehensible thing about the world
is that it is comprehensible.

ALBERT EINSTEIN

Science is organized knowledge.

HERBERT SPENCER
Education

Science is a collection of facts concerning natural
objects or phenomena, arranged in good order, and
made useful.

WILLIAM TEMPLE HORNADAY
The American Natural History

Never, nor in any place, has man governed matter,
unless it be when he has exactly observed its behaviour
and followed its laws with great attention. And
only in so far as he has done this can he govern it and
only just to this extent.

CARL G. JUNG
Psychological Reflections

There is a gulf between the life of the scientist and
the life of a man who isn't actively a scientist,
dangerously deep. The experience of science—to stub
your toe hard and then notice that it was really a rock
on which you stubbed it—this experience is something
that is hard to communicate by popularization, by
education, or by talk. It is almost as hard to tell a man
what it is like to find out something new about the world
as it is to describe a mystical experience to a chap
who has never had any hint of such an experience.

J. ROBERT OPPENHEIMER
The Open Mind

The seeds of great discoveries are constantly
floating around, but they only take root in minds well
prepared to receive them.

JOSEPH HENRY

I have steadily endeavored to keep my mind free
so as to give up any hypothesis, however much beloved
(and I cannot resist forming one on every subject), as
soon as the facts are shown to be opposed to it.

CHARLES DARWIN

I dream up all sorts of theories at night and then
disprove them in the laboratory the next day. Checking
a hunch, sometimes I see some discrepancy, something
unexpected—then I follow it up. Success depends on
whether the hunch was good or bad.

ALBERT SZENT-GYÖRGYI

When you've filled yourself with a particular
problem, . . . you have a great desire to have some
clarity in it. You go through this long, hard period of
filling yourself up with as much information as you can.
You just sort of feel it all rumbling around inside of

you, not particularly at a conscious level. Then . . .
you begin to feel a solution, a resolution, bubbling up to
your consciousness. At the same time you begin to
get very excited, tremendously elated—pervaded by a
fantastic sense of joy.

ROBERT R. WILSON

We saw only very few persons at the laboratory;
among the physicists and chemists there were a few who
came from time to time, either to see our experiments
or to ask for advice. . . . Then took place some
conversations before the blackboard—the sort of
conversation one remembers well because it acts as a
stimulant for scientific interest and the ardor for
work without interrupting the course of reflection and
without troubling that atmosphere of peace and
meditation which is the true atmosphere of a laboratory.

MARIE CURIE

It is not simply that cancer researchers and astronomers
do different things, they talk different languages, tend to
have different personality types; they think,
dress and live differently.

ALVIN TOFFLER
Future Shock

I just don't think nature is very tricky. I don't believe
that one phenomenon or another is an enormous
coincidence, or accident, or just happened to happen.
Everything that is true is very simple, once we
understand it. It's only complicated when we don't.

BERND MATTHIAS

In spite of the difficulties of our working conditions,
we felt very happy. Our days were spent at the
laboratory. In our poor shed there reigned a great

tranquillity; sometimes, as we watched over some
operation, we would walk up and down, talking about
work in the present and in the future; when we were
cold a cup of hot tea taken near the stove comforted
us. We lived in our single preoccupation as
if in a dream.

MARIE CURIE

Biology is beginning to provide us with control over
living matter—new drugs, new methods for fighting
disease, new kinds of animals and plants. It is helping
us also to a new intellectual outlook, in which man
is seen not as a finished being, single lord of creation,
but as one among millions of the products of an
evolution that is still in progress.

JULIAN HUXLEY

Of course no scientist can be continuously aware of
... remote possible consequences of his labors; in
fact the long goal is so remote that if he kept his eye
on it he would become hopelessly discouraged
over the half inch of progress his own life's work will
represent. But it was the vision of this which first made
him choose his curious career, and it is an emotional
sense of the great structure of scientific knowledge to
which his little grain will be added which drives
him along.

OLIVER LA FARGE

In man's technological progress, therefore, it
required tens of centuries to arrive at the idea of
scientific planning and checking. Man made his latest
great step forward when he said, "Just what is it I
want to do?" and then tested his results to see if he had
attained his object. In this way he discovered that
planning could unlock the previously unknown.

RUTH BENEDICT

Science first gave man a sense of mastery over his environment, and hence over the future. By making the future seem malleable, instead of immutable, it shattered the opiate religions that preached passivity and mysticism. Today, mounting evidence that society is out of control breeds disillusionment with science. In consequence, we witness a garish revival of mysticism.

ALVIN TOFFLER
Future Shock

The world of poetry, mythology, and religion represents the world as a man would like to have it, while science represents the world as he gradually comes to discover it.

JOSEPH WOOD KRUTCH
The Modern Temper

Science without religion is lame, religion without science is blind.

ALBERT EINSTEIN

Faith is a fine invention
For gentlemen who see;
But microscopes are prudent
In an emergency.

EMILY DICKINSON

Where the telescope ends, the microscope begins.
Which of the two has the grander view?

VICTOR HUGO
Les Misérables

44. Exploring

I . . . had ambition not only to go farther than any
man had ever been before, but as far as possible for a
man to go . . . .

JAMES COOK

They are ill discoverers that think there is no land,
when they can see nothing but sea.

FRANCIS BACON

I have often heard people say, "I wonder what it would
be like to be on board a spaceship," and the answer is
very simple. What *does* it feel like? That is all you have
ever experienced. You are all astronauts. I am sure
you do not immediately agree and say "Yes, that's right,
I am an astronaut." I am sure that you do not really
sense yourself to be aboard a fantastically real
spaceship—our spherical Spaceship Earth.

R. BUCKMINSTER FULLER
Our Spaceship Earth

From a very young age I began to follow the sea
and have continued to do so to this day. This art of
navigation incites those who pursue it to inquire into the
secrets of this world. I have passed more than forty
years in this business and have traveled to every place
where there is navigation up to the present time. . . . I
found Our Lord very favorable to this my desire, and to

further it He granted me the gift of knowledge. He
made me skilled in seamanship, equipped me
abundantly with the sciences of astronomy, geometry,
and arithmetic, and taught my mind and hand to
draw this sphere and upon it the cities, rivers, mountains,
islands, and ports, each in its proper place. During
this time I have made it my business to read all that has
been written on geography, history, philosophy, and
other sciences. Thus Our Lord revealed to me that it was
feasible to sail from here to the Indies, and placed
in me a burning desire to carry out this plan.

CHRISTOPHER COLUMBUS
Letter to King Ferdinand and Queen Isabella, *1501*

More than once I have come back from the great
frozen spaces, battered and worn and baffled, sometimes
maimed, telling myself I had made my last journey
thither, eager for the society of my kind, the comforts of
civilization and the peace and serenity of home. But
somehow, it was never many months before the old
restless feeling came over me. Civilization began to lose
its zest for me. I began to long for the great white
desolation, the battles with the ice and the gales, the
long, long Arctic night . . . the silence and vastness of
the great, white, lonely North. And back I went
accordingly, time after time after time, until, at last, my
dream of years came true.

ROBERT E. PEARY

My initial feelings were of relief, relief that there were
no more steps to be cut, no more ridges to traverse
and no more humps to tantalize us with hopes of success.
I looked at Tensing and in spite of the goggles and
oxygen mask . . . there was no disguising his infectious
grin of pure delight as he looked all around him. We
shook hands and then Tensing threw his arm round
my shoulders and we thumped each other on the back.

EDMUND HILLARY
describing his conquest of Mount Everest

I started at sunrise and climbed the lower mountain slopes until I came to a small forest. Far from an inhabited place, I had only myself to count on. The solitude suddenly made me feel extremely vulnerable. I had the sensation that my life was in danger. . . . I was part of nature, like an animal among other animals. . . . Finally, worn and hungry, I reached the crest. I had striven against nature like a primitive man to gain that goal, and suddenly I experienced a vast exultancy.

MAURICE HERZOG
Annapurna

O to realize space!
The plenteousness of all, that there are
        no bounds,
To emerge and be of the sky, of the sun
        and moon and flying clouds,
    as one with them.

WALT WHITMAN
"A Song of Joys," Leaves of Grass

Humanity lies in man's urge to explore the world. It lies in man's unique drive to understand the nature of the universe within which he lives. It lies in man's capacity to question the known and imagine the unknown.

MARGARET MEAD
A Way of Seeing

I always had what I think is the natural desire of most pilots to want to go a little bit higher and faster. I thought that we ought to be trying to extend man's capacities up there.

LEROY GORDON COOPER, JR.
We Seven

I thought this was a chance for immortality.
Pioneering in space was something that I would
willingly give my life for. . . . I think a person is very
fortunate to have something in life that he can care
that much about.

MALCOLM SCOTT CARPENTER
We Seven

"What is the news, good neighbor, I pray?"
"They say a balloon has gone up to the moon
And won't be back till a week from today."

NURSERY RHYME
first printed, 1805

The importance of reaching the stars is that somewhere
out there are other life forms and even, in all likelihood,
other intelligences. To study other forms of life or
to make contact with other intelligences would represent
a chance at a monumental advance of knowledge.

ISAAC ASIMOV
"The Next 100 Years," World Almanac, 1968

Conquest has explored more than ever curiosity has
done; and the path of science has been commonly
opened by the sword.

SYDNEY SMITH

Trembling with excitement I watched a world so
new and unknown to me, trying to see and remember
everything. Astonishingly bright cold stars could be
seen through the windows. They were still far away—oh,
how far away—but in orbit they seemed closer than
the Earth. But the point was not the distance . . . but the
principle. Man had overcome the force of Earth's
gravity and gone out into space.

YURI GAGARIN
Survival in Space

"Christopher, Christopher, where are you going,
   Christopher Robin?"

"Just up to the top of the hill,
Upping and upping until
I am right on the top of the hill,"
   said Christopher Robin.

A. A. MILNE
"Journey's End," Now We Are Six

I would have to run to him, only I was a coward in
the presence of such a mob—would have embraced him,
only, being an Englishman, I did not know how he
would receive me; so I did what cowardice and false
pride suggested was the best thing—walked deliberately
to him, took off my hat, and said:
   "Dr. Livingstone, I presume?"
   "Yes," said he, with a kind smile, lifting his cap
slightly.
   I replaced my hat on my head, and he puts on his
cap, and we both grasp hands, and I then say aloud:
   "I thank God, Doctor, I have been permitted to
see you."
   He answered, "I feel thankful that I am here to
welcome you."

HENRY M. STANLEY
How I Found Livingstone, 1872

We explore and we retrench, we investigate and we
stabilize. Step by step we expand our awareness
and understanding both of ourselves and of the complex
environment we live in.

DESMOND MORRIS
The Naked Ape

One of the advantages of being disorderly is that
one is constantly making exciting discoveries.

A. A. MILNE

My heart is warm with the friends I make,
And better friends I'll not be having,
Yet there isn't a train I wouldn't take,
No matter where it's going.

EDNA ST. VINCENT MILLAY
"Travel"

45. Creativity

Once he has touched art, he can never be the same
again. It's like going down a great avenue; he will
always recall it.

LOUISE NEVELSON
The New York Times Magazine, *January 24, 1971*

Who is there so bold as to proclaim that he has defined
art? That he has enumerated all its facets?

ALEKSANDR I. SOLZHENITSYN
Nobel Prize Acceptance Speech, 1972

It is my opinion that art lost its basic creative
drive the moment it was separated from worship. It
severed an umbilical cord and now lives its own sterile
life, generating and degenerating itself. In former
days the artist remained unknown and his work was
to the glory of God.

INGMAR BERGMAN
Introduction, Four Screen Plays

In order for man to get about easily he must pitch
overboard all his art. Straighten out all his roads—cut

down all the trees—level the mountains and fill
up the streams.

JOHN MARIN
John Marin by John Marin

⎯⎯⎯⎯⎯⎯

The genuine creator creates something that has a
life of its own, something that can exist and function
without him. This is true not only of the writer, artist
and scientist, but of creators in other fields. . . .
With the noncreative it is the other way around: in
whatever they do, they arrange things so that
they themselves become indispensable.

ERIC HOFFER
The New York Times Magazine, *April 25, 1971*

⎯⎯⎯⎯⎯⎯

Everyone's got to be different. You can't copy anybody
and end up with anything. If you copy, it means you're
working without any real feeling. And without feeling,
whatever you do amounts to nothing.

BILLIE HOLIDAY
Lady Sings The Blues

⎯⎯⎯⎯⎯⎯

In the creative state a man is taken out of himself.
He lets down as it were a bucket into his subconscious,
and draws up something which is normally beyond
his reach. He mixes this thing with his normal
experiences, and out of this mixture he makes a
work of art.

E. M. FORSTER

⎯⎯⎯⎯⎯⎯

If you paint, close your eyes and sing.

PABLO PICASSO

⎯⎯⎯⎯⎯⎯

The true artist will let his wife starve, his children
go barefoot, his mother drudge for his living at seventy,
sooner than work at anything but his art.

GEORGE BERNARD SHAW
Man and Superman

There's no such thing beneath the heavens as
conditions favourable to art. . . . Art must crash through
or perish, and I simply just crashed through; but not
without wounds, believe me. Take what you want from
life but pay for it in blood.

SYLVIA ASHTON-WARNER
Teacher

The great work of art is great because it creates
a special world of its own. It revives and readapts time
and space, and the measure of its success is the
extent to which it makes you an inhabitant of that
world—the extent to which it invites you in and lets you
breathe its strange, special air.

LEONARD BERNSTEIN
"What Makes Opera Grand?"
Vogue, December 1958

Why did Mozart compose music?

JONAS SALK
on why he has devoted his life to science,
Time, March 29, 1954

Genius is childhood recaptured.

CHARLES BAUDELAIRE

Talent is that which is in a man's power. Genius is
that in whose power a man is.

JAMES RUSSELL LOWELL
Among My Books: Rousseau and the Sentimentalists

All art is a revolt against man's fate.

ANDRÉ MALRAUX
Voices of Silence

The true function of art is to . . . edit nature and so make it coherent and lovely. The artist is a sort of impassioned proofreader, blue-penciling the bad spelling of God.

H. L. MENCKEN

When a work of art appears to be in advance of its period, it is really the period that has lagged behind the work of art.

JEAN COCTEAU

Art is a human activity, consisting in this, that one man consciously, by means of certain external signs, hands on to others feelings he has lived through, and that other people are infected by these feelings and also experience them.

LEO TOLSTOY

Everyone wants to understand art. Why not try to understand the song of a bird? Why does one love the night, flowers, everything around one, without trying to understand them?

PABLO PICASSO

When the film is finished it is never the film I said I wanted to make. . . . It's another thing, another creature, born of certain stimulations and initial conditions, but which has taken on bit by bit a completely different physiognomy.

FEDERICO FELLINI

Art reveals Nature's lack of design, her curious crudities, her absolutely unfinished condition. Nature has good intentions, but she cannot carry them out. Art is our gallant attempt to teach Nature her proper place.

OSCAR WILDE

You come to know a thing by being inside it. You get
an inside view. You step into the skin of the beast and
that, precisely, is what the masked and costumed
dancer does. He puts on the beast.

EDMUND CARPENTER
"Reclassification"

It may sound absurd, but I believe that I am speaking
the truth when I say that I have suffered two kinds
of pain through my characters. I have witnessed
their pain when I am in the act of distorting them, of
falsifying them, and I have witnessed their contempt.
I have suffered pain when I have been unable to get
to the quick of them, when they willfully elude
me, and when they withdraw into the shadows. And
there's a third and rarer pain. That is when the
right word, or the right act jolts them or stills them into
their proper life. When that happens, the pain is
worth having. When that happens, I am ready to take
them into the nearest bar and buy drinks all
around. And I hope they would forgive me my
trespasses against them and do the same for me.

HAROLD PINTER
The New York Times, November 14, 1971

It's an odd idea for someone like me to keep a
diary; not only because I have never done so before, but
because it seems to me that neither I—nor for that
matter anyone else—will be interested in the
unbosomings of a thirteen-year-old schoolgirl. Still,
what does that matter? I want to write, but more than
that, I want to bring out all kinds of things that lie
buried deep in my heart.

ANNE FRANK
The Diary of a Young Girl

236

46. The Arts

What really knocks me out is a book that, when you're all done reading it, you wish the author that wrote it was a terrific friend of yours and you could call him up on the phone whenever you felt like it.

J. D. SALINGER
The Catcher in the Rye

To produce a mighty book, you must choose a mighty theme. No great and enduring volume can ever be written on the flea, though many there be that have tried it.

HERMAN MELVILLE
Moby Dick

A writer's problem does not change. He himself changes and the world he lives in changes but his problem remains the same. It is always how to write truly and, having found what is true, to project it in such a way that it becomes a part of the experience of the person who reads it.

ERNEST HEMINGWAY
The Problems of a Writer in War Time

I'm very fond of the English language. I tease it, and you tease only the things you love.

OGDEN NASH
quoted in obituary, The New York Times, *May 20, 1971*

A writer and nothing else: a man alone in a room
with the English language, trying to get human
feelings right.

JOHN K. HUTCHENS
New York Herald-Tribune, *September 10, 1961*

────────────

A person who publishes a book willfully appears
before the populace with his pants down. . . . If
it is a good book nothing can hurt him. If it is a bad
book, nothing can help him.

EDNA ST. VINCENT MILLAY
Letters of Edna St. Vincent Millay

────────────

Some mystery should be left in the revelation of
character in a play, just as a great deal of mystery
is always left in the revelation of character in
life, even in one's own character to himself.

TENNESSEE WILLIAMS
Stage directions, Cat on a Hot Tin Roof

────────────

The aim of writing is to enable people a little better
to enjoy life or a little better to endure it.

W. H. AUDEN
The New York Times, *December 16, 1970*

────────────

Stories never really end. They can go on and on.
It's just that sometimes, at a certain point, one
stops telling them.

MARY NORTON
The Borrowers

────────────

A novel is a mirror carried along a main road.

HENRI STENDHAL
The Red and the Black

238

There is no iron that can enter the human
heart with such stupefying effect as a period, placed
at the right moment.

ISAAC BABEL

Reading is eye-to-brain, but poetry is
eye-to-ear-to-brain.

CHANDLER M. BROOKS
The New York Times, *December 16, 1970*

If you take two poems by one man and read them
and you can't tell which was written first—that
is a minor poet.

W. H. AUDEN
The New York Times, *December 16, 1970*

Poetry does not consist in saying everything, but in
making one dream everything.

CHARLES SAINTE-BEUVE
"Raphael," Causeries du Lundi

Poetry is concerned with using with abusing,
with losing with wanting, with denying with avoiding,
with adoring with replacing the noun.

GERTRUDE STEIN

Poetry watches life with affection.

MARIANNE MOORE

If I read a book and it makes my whole body so
cold no fire can ever warm me, I know that it is poetry.
If I feel physically as if the top of my head were

taken off, I know it is poetry. These are the only ways
I know it. Is there any other way?

EMILY DICKINSON

Diligence in a poet is the same as dishonesty in a
bookkeeper. There are rafts of bards who are
writing too much, too diligently, and too slyly. Few
poets are willing to wait out their pregnancy—
they prefer to have a premature baby and allow it to
incubate after being safely laid in Caslon
Old Style.

E. B. WHITE
One Man's Meat

We must get rid of our superstitious valuation of texts
and *written* poetry. Written poetry is worth reading once,
and then should be destroyed. Let the dead poets make
way for others.

ANTONIN ARTAUD
The Theater and Its Double

Like a piece of ice on a hot stove the poem must ride
on its own melting.

ROBERT FROST
Preface, Collected Works

Poetry is the spontaneous overflow of powerful
feelings; it takes its origin from emotion recollected in
tranquillity.

WILLIAM WORDSWORTH
Preface, The Lyrical Ballads

Perhaps no person can be a poet, or can even enjoy
poetry, without a certain unsoundness of mind.

THOMAS BABINGTON MACAULAY
Milton

... mad Ireland hurt you into poetry.
Now Ireland has her madness and her
                    weather still,
For poetry makes nothing happen.

                    W. H. AUDEN
                    "In Memory of W. B. Yeats"

───────────

A poem should be equal to:
Not true.
            • • •

A poem should not mean
But be.

                    ARCHIBALD MACLEISH
                    "Ars Poetica"

───────────

There's a music for everything. Didn't you ever hear
the earth spinning? It makes a sound like a humming-
top. Buckingham Palace plays "Rule Britannia"; the River
Thames is a drowsy flute. Dear me, yes! Everything in
the world—trees, rocks and stars and human beings—
they all have their own true music.

                    P. L. TRAVERS
                    Mary Poppins Opens the Door

───────────

Color in music, as in painting, is meaningful
only when it serves the expressive idea.

                    AARON COPLAND

───────────

Sweet sounds, oh, beautiful music, do not cease!
Reject me not into the world again,
With you alone is excellence and peace,
Mankind made plausible, his purpose plain.

                    EDNA ST. VINCENT MILLAY
                    "On Hearing a Symphony of Beethoven"

It will be generally admitted that Beethoven's Fifth
Symphony is the most sublime noise that has ever
penetrated into the ear of man.

E. M. FORSTER
Howard's End

To play great music, you must keep your eyes on
a distant star.

YEHUDI MENUHIN
Reader's Digest, *December, 1953*

I cannot tell you how much I love to play for people.
Would you believe it—sometimes when I sit down to
practice and there is no one else in the room, I have
to stifle an impulse to ring for the elevator man and offer
him money to come in and hear me.

ARTUR RUBINSTEIN
Holiday, *May 1963*

I have five times as many tunes in my head as lyrics.
Every time you settle for a word to express something,
you lose something. At least I can grease on through
with music.

JAMES TAYLOR
The New York Times Magazine, *February 21, 1971*

Dance is the only art of which we ourselves are the
stuff of which it is made.

TED SHAWN
Time, *July 25, 1955*

Dance is life at its most glorious moment.

PEARL LANG
The New York Times, *February 5, 1971*

Dance is of all things the most concentrated expression
of happiness and everyone needs to find happiness,
to search for an ideal escape.

VIOLETTE VERDY
The New York Times, *February 5, 1971*

O body swayed to music, O brightening glance,
How can we know the dancer from the dance?

WILLIAM BUTLER YEATS
"Among School Children"

There are painters who transform the sun into a yellow
spot, but there are others who, thanks to their art and
intelligence, transform a yellow spot into the sun.

PABLO PICASSO

I like the feel of paint—the drag of the brush across
the tooth of the canvas. A painting is something made
of P-A-I-N-T paint oozing over the canvas— . . .

JOHN MARIN
John Marin on John Marin

An actor must lead a life full of interest, beauty,
variety, excitement and enlightenment. He must be
aware not only of what is going on in the large cities,
but also in all outlying parts of the country, in villages,
factories, plants and in the great world centers of
culture. . . . What actors need is a limitless horizon.

CONSTANTIN SERGEYEVICH STANISLAVSKY

You need three things in the theatre—the play, the
actors and the audience, and each must give something.

KENNETH HAIGH
Theatre Arts, *July 1958*

It's the way to get over a deep inferiority complex,
being onstage; you become another person and shed
your own frightened personality.

SHIRLEY BOOTH
New York Journal-American, *October 30, 1956*

I think it's because I get an audience involved,
personally involved in a song—because I'm involved
myself. It's not something I do deliberately; I can't help
myself. If the song is a lament at the loss of love, I get
an ache in my gut, I feel the loss myself, and I cry
out the loneliness, the hurt and the pain that I feel.

FRANK SINATRA
in Playboy Interviews

Look, acting is just a matter of observation, imitation
and communication. That's what it's all about.

GEORGE C. SCOTT
Time, *March 22, 1971*

XV

"Everything Is Related to Everything Else"

47. Ecology

The first law of ecology is that everything is related
to everything else.

BARRY COMMONER

Three billion years ago, life arose upon the earth.
It is the only life in the solar system.

About two million years ago, man appeared. He has
become the dominant species on the earth. All other
living things, animal and plant, live by his sufferance.
He is the custodian of life on earth, and in the solar
system. It's a big responsibility.

GEORGE WALD
The New Yorker, March 22, 1969

I started in killing buffalo for the Union Pacific
Railroad. I had a wagon with four mules, one driver
and two butchers, all brave, well-armed men. . . . It
was my custom in those days to pick out a herd that
seemed to have the fattest cows and young heifers. I
would then rush my horse into them, picking out the
fattest cows and shooting them down, while my horse
would be running along side of them. . . . I have killed
from twenty-five to forty buffalo while the herd was
circling, and they would all be dropped very close
together; that is to say, in a space covering about five
acres. . . . I killed buffalo for the railroad company for
twelve months, and during that time the number I

brought into camp was kept account of, and at the end
of that period I had killed 4,280 buffalo.

"BUFFALO BILL" CODY
True Tales of the Plains

Thank God, men cannot as yet fly, and lay waste the
sky as well as the earth! We are safe on that side for
the present.

HENRY DAVID THOREAU
Journal, *January 3, 1861*

It is not always the other person who pollutes our
streams, or litters our highways, or throws away a
match in a forest, or wipes out game, or wipes out
our fishing reserves.

JOHN F. KENNEDY
*Address at the Pinchot Institute for Conservation
Studies, Milford, Pennsylvania, September 24, 1963*

But Americans, beginning with the three million spread
thinly along the eastern seaboard when we became a
nation, were beguiled by their sense of the boundless
land stretching out beyond the western horizon, which
seemed limitless in its promise of rich resources, and
gave little thought to conserving any part of it
for the future.

MARGARET MEAD
A Way of Seeing

When I hear of the destruction of a species I feel as
if all the works of some great writer had perished.

THEODORE ROOSEVELT
Letter to Frank M. Chapman, *February 15, 1899*

The sun, moon and stars would have disappeared long
ago had they been within the reach of predatory human
hands.

HAVELOCK ELLIS
The Dance of Life

247

To live healthily and successfully on the land, we must also live with it. We must be part not only of the human community, but of the whole community; we must acknowledge some sort of oneness not only with our neighbors, our countrymen and our civilization, but also with the natural as well as the man-made community. Ours is not only "one world" in the sense usually implied by that term; it is also "one earth."

JOSEPH WOOD KRUTCH
The Voice of the Desert

Conquest, or mastery, is neither the only nor the best manner to deal with natural forces. Man should try instead to collaborate with them. Ideally, he should insert himself into the environment in such a manner that his ways of life and technologies make him once more a part of nature.

RENÉ JULES DUBOS

No species except man could so alter the working of ecology relationships that nature could not restore them. In a multitude of places over the centuries man has so altered them that nature's readjustment has been infinitely the worse for him; and sometimes it will require not centuries but geological epochs to restore them to the equivalent of what they were. It may turn out that nuclear fission has enabled him to alter them to the point where no one will have any further interest in the matter.

LEWIS KETCHAM SILLCOX
Lecture, Massachusetts Institute of Technology, February 7, 1956

America today stands poised on a pinnacle of wealth and power, yet we live in a land of vanishing beauty, of increasing ugliness, of shrinking open space, and of an over-all environment that is diminished daily by

pollution and noise and blight. This, in brief, is the quiet
conservation crisis of the 1960's.

STEWART UDALL
The Quiet Crisis

No good citizen or subject can possibly be willing
to permit or condone the *wasteful* and unfair destruction
of wild life, or forests, or grazing lands, and the turning
over of empty deserts and lifeless waste lands as the
heritage of our children's children. Of that, let all
Americans beware. The time for indifference and apathy
toward Conservation has savagely passed.

WILLIAM TEMPLE HORNADAY
The American Natural History

Our national flower is the concrete cloverleaf.

LEWIS MUMFORD
Quote *Magazine, October 8, 1961*

Here is something that the psychologists have so far
neglected: the love of ugliness for its own sake, the
lust to make the world intolerable. Its habitat is the
United States. Out of the melting pot emerges a race
which hates beauty as it hates truth.

H. L. MENCKEN
The Vintage Mencken

Over increasingly large areas of the United States,
spring now comes unheralded by the return of the birds,
and the early mornings are strangely silent where
once they were filled with the beauty of bird song.

RACHEL CARSON
Silent Spring

What's one more candy wrapper on a city street? . . .
Just add one more soft-drink can . . . one more bit

of orange peel . . . one more matchbook . . . one more
cigar butt . . . you can build a mountain of garbage
in no time.

THE AMERICAN MUSEUM OF NATURAL HISTORY, NEW YORK
Handbook to exhibit Can Man Survive?, *1969*

Perhaps the most important message of ecology
is the concept that man must master the conditions of
life in order to survive.

MURRAY BOOKCHIN

If allowed to survive this grass will produce
enough oxygen for two students to breathe for one
semester.

*Sign on lawn, University of Iowa,
photograph in* The New York Times, *May 30, 1971*

Man is endowed with reason and creative force to
increase what has been given him; but hitherto he has
not created but destroyed. There are fewer and
fewer forests, the rivers are drying up, the wild
creatures are becoming extinct, the climate is ruined,
and every day the earth is growing poorer and
more hideous.

ANTON CHEKHOV
Uncle Vanya

Conservation means development as much as it
does protection. I recognize the right and duty of this
generation to develop and use the natural resources
of our land; but I do not recognize the right to
waste them, or to rob, by wasteful use, the generations
that come after us. I ask nothing of the nation except
that it so behave as each farmer here behaves with
reference to his own children. That farmer is a
poor creature who skins the land and leaves it
worthless to his children.

THEODORE ROOSEVELT
The New Nationalism

The generation now living may well be that which
will make the irrevocable decision whether or not
America will continue to be for centuries to come the
one great nation which had the foresight to preserve
an important part of its heritage.

JOSEPH WOOD KRUTCH

The opportunity to see wild geese is more important
than television, and the chance to find a pasque-flower
is a right as inalienable as free speech.

ALDO LEOPOLD
A Sand County Almanac

I think that I shall never see
A billboard lovely as a tree.
Perhaps unless the billboards fall,
I'll never see a tree at all.

OGDEN NASH
"Song of the Open Road"

Indeed, Western society is in the process of
completing the rape and murder of the planet for
economic gain. And, sadly, most of the rest of the world
is eager for the opportunity to emulate our behavior.
But the underdeveloped peoples will be denied that
opportunity—the days of plunder are drawing
inexorably to a close.

PAUL EHRLICH

Hurt not the earth, neither the sea, nor the trees.

REVELATION 7:3

48. Nature

There is a pleasure in the pathless woods,
There is a rapture on the lonely shore,
There is society, where none intrudes,
By the deep sea, and music in its roar:
I love not man the less, but Nature more.

LORD BYRON
Childe Harold's Pilgrimage

On the trail marked with pollen may I walk
With grasshoppers about my feet may I walk
With dew about my feet may I walk
With beauty may I walk.

AMERICAN INDIAN POEM

I go to Nature to be soothed and healed, and to
have my senses put in tune once more.

JOHN BURROUGHS
Time and Change

I want to go fishing! somewhere
 on a stream
I want to give way to the longing
 to a dream.
Away from the tumult of motor and mill
I want to be care-free; I want to be
 still!

I'm weary of doing things; weary of
  words
I want to be one with the blossoms
  and birds.

EDGAR A. GUEST
"Hunger"

To be part of summer one must feel a part of life,
but to be part of winter one must feel a part of
something older than life itself.

JOSEPH WOOD KRUTCH
The Twelve Seasons

The shore is an ancient world, for as long as there
has been an earth and sea there has been this place
of the meeting of land and water. Yet it is a world
that keeps alive the sense of continuing creation and of
the relentless drive of life. Each time that I enter
it, I gain some new awareness of its beauty and its
deeper meanings, sensing that intricate fabric of
life by which one creature is linked with another, and
each with its surroundings.

RACHEL CARSON
The Edge of the Sea

I have yet to find evidence that nature has
any motive beyond the insistence of life itself. There
certainly is neither charity nor malevolence in nature,
nor any degree of either punishment or pardon.
Rain falls on the just and the unjust alike, and so does
hail. . . . Despite man's long habit of endowing sun,
moon, stars, weather, and other natural elements and
forces with anthropomorphic passions and sensibilities,
it is my experience that the patterns of nature's
behavior are quite unrelated to man's wishes, his
needs, or even his prayers.

HAL BORLAND
Countryman

Each mile took us farther and farther into the
unsettled prairie until in the afternoon of the second
day, we came to a meadow so wide that its western
rim touched the sky without revealing a sign of
man's habitation other than the road in which we
travelled.

The plain was covered with grass tall as ripe
wheat and when my father stopped his team and came
back to us and said, "Well, children, here we are
on the Big Prairie," we looked about us with awe, so
endless seemed this spread of wild oats and
waving blue-joint.

HAMLIN GARLAND
A Son of the Middle Border

The wind had dropped, and the snow, tired of
rushing round in circles trying to catch itself up, now
fluttered gently down until it found a place on
which to rest, and sometimes the place was Pooh's
nose and sometimes it wasn't, and in a little while
Piglet was wearing a white muffler round his neck and
feeling more snowy behind the ears than he had
ever felt before.

A. A. MILNE
The House at Pooh Corner

I would not willingly give up our four seasons
for a Kingdom of Heaven in which the sun shone
eternally with equal warmth and light, in which the
grass was forever green and the birds sang
constantly. . . . Nothing is precious without a degree of
rarity. Be warned that in the land of eternal spring
you will find the inhabitants blind and deaf.

LOUIS J. HALLE
Spring in Washington

I know a bank where the wild thyme blows,
Where ox-lips and the nodding violet grows;

Quite over-canopied with lush woodbine,
With sweet musk-roses and with eglantine.

WILLIAM SHAKESPEARE
A Midsummer Night's Dream, II:1

Nothing more beautiful under the sun than to be under
the sun.

INGEBORG BACHMAN
"To the Sun"

When I was a boy, and saw bright rows of icicles
In many lengths along a wall
I was disappointed to find
That I could not play music upon them:
I ran my hand lightly across them
And they fell, tinkling.
I tell you this, young man, so that your
       expectations of life
Will not be too great.

CONRAD AIKEN
"Improvisations: Light and Snow"

Did you ever take pencil and book to scribe down
the sounds the wind makes as it sifts and soughs
through trees? Each kind of tree is a sort of musical
instrument: the apple a cello, the old oak a bass
viol, the cypress a harp, the willow a flute, the young
pine a muted violin. Put your ear close to the
whispering branch and you may catch what it is saying.

GUY MURCHIE, JR.
Song of the Sky

The seasons! If we could understand them, not
scientifically but spiritually, if we knew why they
come so silently and why they are so forceful, might we
not analyze the essence of immortal life. Although
we hastily regard them as a thing apart from ourselves,

255

we are really united to them closely. . . . Winter,
spring, summer and autumn regulate our lives;
willy-nilly, they govern our daily and yearly progress.
We have not yet come so far from primeval nature
that we can remain indifferent to them.

BROOKS ATKINSON
East of the Hudson

On the farm the weather was the great fact and
men's affairs went on underneath it, as the streams
creep under the ice.

WILLA CATHER
My Antonia

I frequently tramped eight or ten miles through
the deepest snow to keep an appointment with a beech-
tree, or a yellow birch, or an old acquaintance among
the pines.

HENRY DAVID THOREAU
"Winter Visitors," Walden

To me a lush carpet of pine needles or spongy grass
is more welcome than the most luxurious Persian rug.
To me the pageant of seasons is a thrilling and
unending drama, the action of which streams through
my fingertips.

HELEN KELLER

A forest is more than an area covered by trees. In
many ways, it is like a city—nature's city—constructed
and peopled with trees, birds, insects, shrubs, mammals,
herbs, snails, ferns, spiders, fungi, mosses, mites,
bacteria, and a myriad of other living forms.

JACK MC CORMICK
The Living Forest

The grass lives, goes to sleep, lives again, and has no
  name for it.
The oaks and poplars know seasons while standing to
  take what comes.

CARL SANDBURG
"The People, Yes"

The sea is always the same:
and yet the sea always changes.

CARL SANDBURG
"North Atlantic"

O for the voices of animals—O for the
  swiftness and balance of fishes!
O for the dropping of raindrops in a song!
O for the sunshine and motion of waves in a
  song!

WALT WHITMAN
"A Song of Joys," Leaves of Grass

A man who never sees a bluebird only half lives.

LEWIS GANNETT
Cream Hill

All through the summer
I wanted to be an engine driver
But after the rain
I wanted to be a Beatle.

MIKE EVANS

It becomes necessary occasionally, simply to throw
open the hatches and ventilate one's psyche, or
whatever you choose to call it. This means an excursion
to some place where the sky is not simply what you
see at the end of the street.

LOUIS J. HALLE
Spring in Washington

Where is Anne?
Head above the buttercups,
Walking by the stream,
Down among the buttercups.
Where is Anne?
Walking with her man,
Lost in a dream,
        Lost among the buttercups.

A. A. MILNE
"Buttercup Days," Now We Are Six

49. Animals

In a world that seems so very puzzling is it any wonder birds have such appeal? Birds are, perhaps, the most eloquent expression of reality.

ROGER TORY PETERSON
Birds Over America

To assume that every wild beast and bird is a sacred creature, peacefully dwelling in an earthly paradise, is a mistake. They have their wisdom and their folly, their joys and their sorrows, their trials and tribulations.

WILLIAM TEMPLE HORNADAY
The American Natural History

We have as good evidence that animals know not only pleasure and pain but also some kind of gladness

and some kind of sorrow, as we have that our human
companions know them.

JOSEPH WOOD KRUTCH
Great American Nature Writing

Dogs are upright as a steeple
And much more loyal than people.
Well people may be reprehensibler
But that's probably because they
   are sensibler.

OGDEN NASH
"An Introduction to Dogs"

The great pleasure of a dog is that you may make a
fool of yourself with him and not only will he not scold
you, but he will make a fool of himself too.

SAMUEL BUTLER
Notebooks

"John, how can you expect sick people to come and
see you when you keep all these animals in the house?
It's a fine doctor would have his parlor full of hedgehogs
and mice! . . . If you go on like this, none of the best
people will have you for a doctor."

"But I like the animals better than the 'best people,' "
said the Doctor.

"You are ridiculous," said his sister, and walked out
of the room.

HUGH LOFTING
The Story of Doctor Doolittle

Animals are such agreeable friends—they ask no
questions, they pass no criticisms.

GEORGE ELIOT
Scenes of Clerical Life

The woes and worries of mankind are enough to
make millions of good people wish that they could

259

take to the woods, and live peacefully among wild
animals that respect the rights of the weak and helpless,
never quarrel over territory, and do not manufacture nor
distribute aerial bombs or poison gas. The more we study
the minds and manners of wild animals, and the more
we interview wild animals, the more do we see by
contrast to admire.

WILLIAM TEMPLE HORNADAY
The American Natural History

Bird watching became a respectable pursuit in New
England long before it was countenanced elsewhere.
It is a hobby that seldom thrives where men are
pushing frontiers; it takes hold when life has settled
down to the civilized complexities. The appeal of birds
seems to be greater the more life is restrained.

ROGER TORY PETERSON
Birds Over America

More than any other creature, the octopus is the spirit
of the reef; unreal themselves, completely fantastic,
unbelievable, weird, they are fitting residents of a world
in which all accepted routines are nullified, in which
animals play at being vegetables, where the trees are
made of brittle stone, where crabs pretend to be things
they are not, where flowers devour fishes, where fishes
imitate sand and rocks and where danger lurks in an
innocent color or harmless shape. That they should,
also, be inhabitants of the shadowy night place is the
final touch on their characters. The octopi fill a niche
of creation claimed by no others and a niche which
they occupy to perfection.

GILBERT C. KLINGEL
Inagua

I try to handle these creatures (grass snakes) as little
as possible. I do not want to steal them from themselves

by making them pets. The exchange of hearts would
degrade both of us. It is only that they are nice. Nice
to see the strange wild things loose, living their ancient
unpredictable lives with such grace. They are more
ancient than the mammoth, and infinitely more beautiful.
They are dry, cool and strong. The fitting and variation
of the plates, the lovely colouring, the movement, their
few thoughts: one could meditate upon them like a
jeweller for months.

T. H. WHITE

The silence of the snowy aisles of the forest, the
whirring flight of partridges, the impudent bark of
squirrels, the quavering voices of owls and coons, the
music of the winds in the high trees—all these
impressions unite in my mind like parts of a woodland
symphony. I soon learned to distinguish the raccoon's
mournful call from the quavering cry of the owl, and
I joined the hired man in hunting rabbits from under
the piles of brush in the clearing. Once or twice some
ferocious, larger animal, possibly a panther, hungrily
yowled in the impenetrable thickets to the north, but this
only lent a still more enthralling interest to the forest.

HAMLIN GARLAND
A Son of the Middle Border

So that was the way the Doctor came to know that
animals had a language of their own and could talk
to one another. And all that afternoon, while it was raining, Polynesia sat on the kitchen table giving him bird
words to put down in the book.

At tea-time, when the dog, Jip, came in, the parrot said
to the Doctor, "See, *he's* talking to you."

"Looks to me as though he were scratching his ear,"
said the Doctor.

"But animals don't always speak with their mouths,"
said the parrot in a high voice, raising her eyebrows.
"They talk with their ears, with their feet, with their

tails—with everything. Sometimes they don't *want* to
make a noise. Do you see now the way he's twitching
up one side of his nose?"

"What's that mean?" asked the Doctor.

"That means, 'Can't you see that it has stopped
raining?' " Polynesia answered. "He is asking you a
question. Dogs nearly always use their noses for asking
questions."

HUGH LOFTING
The Story of Doctor Doolittle

───────────

I never saw a wild thing
Sorry for itself.

D. H. LAWRENCE
"Self-Pity"

───────────

And Saint Francis rejoiced with them, and was glad,
and marvelled much at so great a company of birds
and their most beautiful diversity and their good heed
and sweet friendliness, for which cause he devoutly
praised their Creator in them.

ANONYMOUS
The Little Flowers of St. Francis of Assisi *(14th century)*

───────────

When a man wants to murder a tiger he calls it sport;
when the tiger wants to murder him he calls it
ferocity.

GEORGE BERNARD SHAW
The Revolutionist's Handbook

───────────

Little cat, are you as glad to have me to
     lie upon
As I am to feel your fur under my hand?

AMY LOWELL
"After An Illness (To a Cat from whom
one has been separated for a long time)"

262

XVI

"I Can't Stop Eating Peanuts"

50. Film and Television

I hate television. I hate it as much as peanuts.
But I can't stop eating peanuts.

ORSON WELLES
New York Herald-Tribune, *October 12, 1956*

A nation . . . has permitted a communications system
of such potential to develop into so miserable and
dangerous a contraption.

ERIC F. GOLDMAN
The New York Times Book Review, *November 21, 1971*

Films, much like literature and drama, come out of our
society and mirror it, and beyond matters of clothing
and interior decoration, movies reflect and do not set
patterns.

JUDITH CRIST
Look, *January 9, 1968*

It is always a game when making a film, to see if you
can take from life, from reality, in order to produce the
illusion of reality.

DESIRÉ ECARRÉ
The New York Times, *November 9, 1972*

The film's job is to make the audience "help itself," not to "entertain" it. To grip, not to amuse. To furnish the audience with cartridges, not to dissipate the energies that it brought into the theater.

SERGEI EISENSTEIN
Film Form

Film has nothing to do with literature; the character and substance of the two art forms are usually in conflict. This probably has something to do with the receptive process of the mind. The written word is read and assimilated by a conscious act of the will in alliance with the intellect; little by little it affects the imagination and the emotions. The process is different with a motion picture. When we experience a film, we consciously prime ourselves for illusion. Putting aside will and intellect, we make way for it in our imagination. The sequence of pictures plays directly on our feelings.

INGMAR BERGMAN
Introduction, Four Screen Plays of Ingmar Bergman

For the movie is the imagination of mankind in acton.

GILBERT SELDES

What this generation was bred to at television's knee was not wisdom but cynicism.

PAULINE KAEL
I Lost It at the Movies

The celebrity is usually nothing greater than a more publicized version of us. . . . He has been fabricated on purpose to satisfy our exaggerated expectations of human greatness. . . . [Celebrities] are nothing but ourselves seen in a magnifying mirror.

DANIEL J. BOORSTIN

Nothing is as fleeting as a moment of wit on television.

DAVID STEINBERG
The New York Times Magazine *April 25, 1971*

A good general conversation is a lovely concept, but there is less and less of it going around. . . . Indeed, it is virtually a spectator sport now. Just dial your favorite panel show and see.

PEG BRACKEN
Family Circle, *November 1971*

The family has been re-structured into a miniature audience, and the home into a miniature theater, modeled on the movie house.

GUNTHER ANDERS
Mass Media Anthology

Television creates its own events, something even the most imaginative newspaper reporter cannot do. The newspaperman can only create words, and however powerful they may be, words do not *happen* over the breakfast table as television *happens* in a living room.

HENRY FAIRLIE
"Can You Believe Your Eyes?",
Horizon, *Spring 1967*

The influence exerted by the television screen is centrifugal. The seats in front of the screen are so arranged that the members of the family no longer face each other. . . . They are no longer together, they are merely placed one beside the other, as mere spectators.

GUNTHER ANDERS
Mass Media Anthology

Screenwriting involves more than mere dialogue and plot. The choice between a closeup and a long-shot, for example, may quite often transcend the plot. If the story of Little Red Riding Hood is told with the wolf in close-up and Little Red Riding Hood in a long shot, the director is concerned primarily with the emotional problems of a wolf with a compulsion to eat little girls. If Little Red Riding Hood is in close-up and the Wolf in long-shot, the emphasis is shifted to the emotional problems of vestigial virginity in a wicked world. Thus, two different stories are being told with the same basic anecdotal material.

ANDREW SARRIS
Interviews with Film Directors

51. Comedy and Humor

You may estimate your capacity for comic perception by being able to detect the ridicule of them you love without loving them less; and more by being able to see yourself ridiculous in dear eyes, and accepting the correction their image of you proposes.

GEORGE MEREDITH
An Essay on Comedy

Comedy is sympathy.

BERT LAHR
in Notes on a Cowardly Lion by John Lahr

Laughter and tears are meant to turn the wheels of the same sensibility: one is wind-power and the other water-power, that is all.

OLIVER WENDELL HOLMES
The Autocrat of the Breakfast-Table

A comedian has to gain more than just a laughing action. The audience must laugh *with* him. The comedian that just has you laugh *at* him very seldom becomes a great comedian. The audience has to root for him. The audience has to sympathize with him. The audience must work for him. Of course, the comedian has to be funny, too.

HAROLD LLOYD

Running around the outside of an insane society, the healthiest thing you can do is laugh.

WARREN HINCKLE
"A Social History of the Hippies," Ramparts, 1967

He deserves paradise who makes his companions laugh.

THE KORAN

There is a comic road to wisdom, as well as a tragic road. There is a comic as well as a tragic control of life. And the comic control may be more usable, more relevant to the human condition in all its normalcy and confusion; its many unreconciled directions. Comedy as well as tragedy can tell us that the vanity of the world is foolishness before the gods.

WILLIE SYPHER
The Meanings of Comedy

Who knows where you draw a line between comedy and tragedy? Take a funeral, for instance: the most solemn occasion. Everyone in black; tears, flowers, handkerchiefs. And then a little man arrives rather late, very breathless. He sneaks into church and sits down beside a very fat man who gives him a perishing look. Nervously, he moves up a seat and sits on somebody's hat. In no time, it's an hilarious comedy.

CHARLES CHAPLIN
in Interviews with Film Directors

Everything is funny as long as it is happening to somebody else.

WILL ROGERS

Comedy is the last refuge of the non-conformist mind.

GILBERT SELDES
The New Republic, *December 20, 1954*

A joke's a very serious thing.

CHARLES CHURCHILL
The Ghost

No man who has once heartily and wholly laughed can be altogether irreclaimably bad.

THOMAS CARLYLE
Sartor Resartus

My guess is that there aren't a hundred top-flight professional comedians, male and female, in the whole world. They are a much rarer and far more valuable commodity than all the gold and precious stones in the world. But because we are laughed at, I don't think people really understand how essential we are to their sanity. If it weren't for the brief respite we give the world with our foolishness, the world would see mass suicide in numbers that compare favorably with the death rate of lemmings.

GROUCHO MARX
Groucho and Me

I have often thought that the funniest gag in the world could be made out of the coronation of a king —if it were not for the expense.

I can imagine how a king would be coming down the street on the way to be crowned, with the life guards and the brass bands and the carriages, with outriders,

and all. But when he gets to the palace where the coronation is to take place, he can't get in. The janitor comes
out and searches frantically for the door key. Can't find
it. His wife has been pressing his pants with the family
flatiron and forgot to put the key back into his pocket.
So the King and all the royalty have to wait until the
janitor hot-foots it home to ask the wife what she did
with the stuff in his pockets when she ironed his pants.

That's the very essence of comedy. That's the stuff it
is made of—contrast and catastrophe involving the
unseating of dignity.

MACK SENNETT

And to love comedy you must know the real world,
and know men and women well enough not to expect
too much of them, though you may still hope for good.

GEORGE MEREDITH
An Essay on Comedy

One inch of joy surmounts of grief a span,
Because to laugh is proper to the man.

RABELAIS
"To the Reader"

Laughter is both an act of protest and an act of
acceptance.

There is joy in the fact that we are all in the same
boat, that there are no exceptions made. On the other
hand, we cannot help wishing that we had no problems.

W. H. AUDEN
The New York Times, February 2, 1971

Humor—the ability to laugh at life—is right at the top,
with love and communication, in the hierarchy of our
needs. Humor has much to do with pain; it exaggerates

the anxieties and absurdities we feel, so that we gain
distance and, through laughter, relief.

SARA DAVIDSON
"A Funny Man for This Season,"
The New York Times Magazine, *April 25, 1971*

There is nothing so illiberal and so ill-bred as audible
laughter. I am sure that since I have had the full use
of my reason, nobody has ever heard me laugh.

LORD CHESTERFIELD
Letters, March 9, 1748

52. Sports

The pleasure of sport was so often the chance to
indulge the cessation of time itself—the pitcher dawdling
on the mound, the skier poised at the top of a mountain
trail, the basketball player with the rough skin of the
ball against his palm preparing for a foul shot, the tennis
player at set point over his opponent—all of them
savoring a moment before commiting themselves to
action.

GEORGE PLIMPTON
Paper Lion

Interest and proficiency in almost any one activity—
swimming, boating, fishing, skiing, skating—breed
interest in many more. Once someone discovers the
delight of mastering one skill, however slightly, he is
likely to try out not just one more, but a whole ensemble.

MARGARET MEAD
A Way of Seeing

The temperament which inclines men to sports is
essentially a boyish temperament. The addiction to
sports, therefore, in a peculiar degree marks an arrested
development of the man's moral nature.

THORSTEIN VEBLEN

Eighteen men play a game of baseball and eighteen
thousand watch them, and yet those who play are
the only ones who have an official direction in the
matter of rules and regulations. The eighteen thousand
are allowed to run wild.

ROBERT BENCHLEY

Americans believe in the happy ending. It is hard to
make them accept the fact that if two football teams meet
one of them is pretty sure to lose. The American goes into
sport as he goes into war, expecting, of course, to win.

JOHN R. TUNIS
The American Way in Sports

I don't think winning is the most important thing. I
think it's the only thing.

JIM TATUM
football coach, University of North Carolina

Playing basketball is not reality. People do things
for the player they wouldn't do for others. He is not
prepared to come down to earth. When he leaves some
jive college he never should have gone to in the first
place, no degree, no more dream of playing pro ball,
what's he got? Drugs, maybe. It's all part of this
fanatical emphasis on winning. Ridiculous.

RONNIE HAIGLER
The New York Times, *April 26, 1971*

Pride has always been very important to me. I love to win. It's the one thing that's stayed with me from the beginning.

BILL RUSSELL

More often than not, football is luck. You can study the defense and call a play that you think'll kill 'em, and all of a sudden they put on a line slant that squashes the play. It occurred to me that a lot of the success or failure depended upon the luck of the situation.

FRANK RYAN
in Dr. Ryan of the Browns by Jack Olsen

They said I lacked the killer instinct—which was also true. I found no joy in knocking people unconscious or battering their faces. . . . I had a notion that the killer instinct was really founded in fear, that the killer of the ring raged with ruthless brutality because deep down he was afraid.

GENE TUNNEY
"My Fights With Jack Dempsey"
in The Aspirin Age

My purpose was to become heavyweight champion of the world. Everything I do has a purpose; all of God's beings have a purpose. But only one out of 200 knows what the purpose is. . . . Only that one man knows what happiness is. The other may know pleasure, but pleasure is not happiness. It has no more importance than a shadow following a man.

MUHAMMAD ALI
Life, March 5, 1971

In a fight, you know, when a man has you where he wants you, he is going to deliver the best goods he has.

JAMES J. CORBETT
Roar of the Crowd

The whole method of surf-riding and surf-fighting, I learned, is one of nonresistance. Dodge the blow that is struck at you. Dive through the wave that is trying to slap you in the face. Sink down, feet first, deep under the surface, and let the big smoker that is trying to smash you go far overhead. Never be rigid. Relax. Yield yourself to the waters that are ripping and tearing at you. When the undertow catches you and drags you seaward along the bottom, don't struggle against it. If you do, you are liable to be drowned, for it is stronger than you. Yield yourself to that undertow. Swim with it, not against it, and you will find the pressure removed.

JACK LONDON
The Cruise of the Snark

The days are all too short when one goes fishing. This is true even when the fates are unkind and luck against us.

THEODORE GORDON
"Little Talks About Fly Fishing"
in The Realm of Sport

Speed-skating is only a kind of running on skates, but in hockey the skates of the player are so integrated with his body and brain that they become a part of his personality. The good hockey player never lurches, strains or runs. Watch him closely and see how he glides.

HUGH MAC LENNAN
The Winter Game

Hunting for a day or two without finding game, where the work is severe and toilsome, is a good test of the sportsman's staying qualities; the man who at the end of the time is proceeding with as much caution and determination as at the beginning, has got the right stuff in him.

THEODORE ROOSEVELT
Hunting Trips of a Ranchman

... A man in the woods, with a gun in his hand, is
no longer a man—he is a brute. The devil is in the
gun to make brutes of us all.

JOHN BURROUGHS
Riverby

The nature of tennis and its demands usually make
a good player out of a fellow who has trouble
playing any other game, including tiddlywinks.

BOB CONSIDINE

I can't take much credit for what I did running with a
football, because I don't know what I did. Nobody
ever taught me, and I can't teach anyone. You can
teach a man how to block or tackle or kick or pass. The
ability to run with a ball is something you have or
you haven't. If you can't explain it, how can you take
any credit for it?

RED GRANGE

Of all the competitive sports, a strong case can be
made for skiing as the most emotional, the most exciting,
the most satisfying. It may be the most difficult of all
sports. Victory, then, is so much sweeter.

MAURY ALLEN
The Record Breakers

For the qualified citizens of the world of international
ski racing must have two prerequisites: skill—and
courage. It takes courage to use skill, or to use it to that
utmost which wins races. A watch-tick moment of
bad judgment, a split second of uncontrol can send a
downhill racer flying off the beaten track at a fatal
60 m.p.h. clip.

DOUG KENNEDY

275

But once I got away from my family and out in the world, I saw what there was and I wanted some of it. And football was the only way I could get to see anything. So I went for that.

DEACON JONES
in Life in the Pit—The Deacon Jones Story by Bill Libby

When I look back, the greatest thing that ever happened to me is that when I first picked up a basketball, I was terrible. If things come naturally, you may not bother to work at improving them and you can fall short of your potential.

BOB PETTIT

What is this thing called basketball? It is, first of all, a game, a sport, next, a business; finally, a disease. It is also color, drama and excitement in the lives of millions of small-town Americans, many of whom lack art galleries, symphonies, books, and the theater in their daily lives. In these small towns in winter basketball dominates the whole place. On Friday nights, when there are games, nothing else takes place. The whole town stops.

JOHN R. TUNIS
The American Way in Sports

It (baseball) is the national pastime. It is youth, springtime, a trip to the country, part of our past. It is the roaring excitement of huge urban crowds and the sleepy green afternoon silences of mid-summer. Without effort, it engenders and thrives on heroes. For six months of the year, it intrudes cheerfully into every American home, then frequently rises to a point of nearly insupportable tension and absorption, and concludes in the happy explosion of the country's favorite sporting spectacle, the World Series.

ROGER ANGELL

The pressure was enormous. Some days I would open my hotel door and there were fifty kids waiting outside my room for autographs. I bet I got to know more back exits to hotels than any man in the world.

JOE DIMAGGIO

It takes a great deal to play this game (football). It takes a lot of pride and a lot of determination and a lot of hustle and a lot of sacrifice, and you have to be in the right frame of mind. You can't do it halfway.

JERRY KRAMER
Instant Replay

XVII

"Let There Be Light"

53. Belief in God

In the beginning God created the Heaven and the
earth. And the earth was without form, and void;
and darkness was upon the face of the deep. And the
Spirit of God moved upon the the face of the waters.
And God said, Let there be light; and there was light.

GENESIS 1:1

And God hath spread the earth as a carpet for you,
that ye may walk therein through spacious paths.

THE KORAN

Let me enjoy the earth no less
Because the all-enacting Might
That fashioned forth its loveliness
Had other aims than my delight.

THOMAS HARDY
"Let Me Enjoy"

He prayeth best, who loveth best
All things both great and small;
For the dear God who loveth us,
He made and loveth all.

SAMUEL TAYLOR COLERIDGE
"The Rime of the Ancient Mariner"

I would rather live in a world where my life is
surrounded by mystery than live in a world so
small that my mind could comprehend it.

HARRY EMERSON FOSDICK
"The Mystery of Life," Riverside Sermons

The chess-board is the world, the pieces are the
phenomena of the universe, the rules of the game are
what we call the laws of Nature. The player on the
other side is hidden from us. We know that his play is
always fair, just, and patient. But also we know,
to our cost, that he never overlooks a mistake, or
makes the smallest allowance for ignorance.

T. H. HUXLEY
A Liberal Education

To me every hour of the light, and dark is a miracle,
Every cubic inch of space is a miracle.

WALT WHITMAN
"Miracles," Leaves of Grass

Though he slay me, yet will I trust in him.

JOB 13:15

I had never been truly in solitary confinement;
God's companionship does not stop at the door
of a jail cell.

MARTIN LUTHER KING, JR.
Why We Can't Wait

I think there's probably a God-shaped hole in
everybody's being. Even if God only exists in people's
minds, He's still a force. I believe in God, and I believe
in Jesus, as a man, a metaphor and a phenomenon.

JAMES TAYLOR
The New York Times Magazine, *February 21, 1971*

The desire of the moth for the star,
Of the night for the morrow,
The devotion to something afar
From the sphere of our sorrow.

PERCY BYSSHE SHELLEY
"To———: One Word Is Too Often Profaned"

Every day is a miracle. The world gets up in the morning and is fed and goes to work, and in the evening it comes home and is fed again and perhaps has a little amusement and goes to sleep. To make that possible, so much has to be done by so many people that, on the face of it, it is impossible. Well, every day we do it; and every day, come hell, come high water, we're going to have to go on doing it as well as we can.

JAMES GOULD COZZENS

When I touch that flower, I am not merely touching that flower. I am touching infinity. That little flower existed long before there were human beings on this earth. It will contrive to exist for thousands, yes, millions of years to come.

GEORGE WASHINGTON CARVER

To everything there is a season, and a time to every purpose under the heaven:
A time to be born, and a time to die; a time to plant, and a time to pluck up that which is planted;
A time to kill, and a time to heal; a time to break down, and a time to build up;
A time to weep, and a time to laugh; a time to mourn, and a time to dance;
A time to cast away stones, and a time to gather stones together; a time to embrace, and a time to refrain from embracing;
A time to get, and a time to lose; a time to keep, and a time to cast away;

A time to rend, and a time to sew; a time to keep
silence, and a time to speak;
A time to love, and a time to hate; a time of war, and
a time of peace.

ECCLESIASTES 3:1–8

O world, I cannot hold thee close enough!
Thy winds, thy wide gray skies!
Thy mists that roll and rise!

EDNA ST. VINCENT MILLAY
"God's World"

Keep cool: it will be all one a hundred years hence.

RALPH WALDO EMERSON

"What's miraculous about a spider's web?" said
Mrs. Arable. "I don't see why you say a web is
a miracle—it's just a web."
"Ever try to spin one?" asked Mr. Dorian.

E. B. WHITE
Charlotte's Web

I think a human being has got to have some faith,
or at least he's got to seek faith. Otherwise his life
will be empty, empty. . . . How can you live
and not know why the cranes fly, why children are
born, why the stars shine in the sky! . . . You must
either know why you live, or else . . . nothing
matters . . . everything's just wild grass . . .

ANTON CHEKHOV
Three Sisters

God is that indefinable something which we all
feel but which we do not know. To me God is
truth and love, God is ethics and morality, God is

283

fearlessness, God is the source of light and
life and yet He is above and beyond all these.
God is conscience. He is even the atheism of the atheist.

MOHANDAS K. GANDHI

True godliness does not turn men out of the world,
but enables them to live better in it and excites
their endeavors to mend it.

WILLIAM PENN

Whether or not it is clear to you, no doubt the universe
is unfolding as it should.

MAX EHRMANN
Desiderata

The sun will set without thy assistance.

THE TALMUD

The truly religious person, if he follows the
essence of the monotheistic idea, does not pray for
anything, does not expect anything from God;
he does not love God as a child loves his father or
mother; he has acquired the humility of sensing
his limitations, to the degree of knowing that he knows
nothing about God. God becomes to him a symbol
in which man, at an earlier stage of his evolution,
has expressed the totality of that which man is
striving for, the realm of the spiritual world,
of love, truth and justice. He has faith in the
principles which "God" represents.

ERICH FROMM
The Art of Loving

Lord, when I look at lovely things which pass,
    Under old trees the shadow of young leaves

Dancing to please the wind along the grass,
  Or the gold stillness of the August sun on
        the August sheaves;
Can I believe there is a heavenlier world than this?

CHARLOTTE MEW
"For the Fields"

Little lamb, who made thee?
Dost thou know who made thee?
Gave thee life, and bid thee feed
By the stream and O'er the mead;
Gave thee clothing of delight,
Softest clothing, woolly, bright.

WILLIAM BLAKE
"The Lamb," Songs of Innocence

The world is charged with the grandeur of God.

GERARD MANLEY HOPKINS
"God's Grandeur"

The best way to know God is to love many things.

VINCENT VAN GOGH

Love is God, and to die means that I, a particle
of love, shall return to the general and eternal
source.

LEO TOLSTOY
War and Peace

I turned to speak to God
  About the world's despair;
But to make bad matters worse
  I found God wasn't there.

ROBERT FROST
"Not All There"

I had rather believe all the fables in the
Legend and the Talmud and the Alcoran than
that this universal frame is without a mind.

> FRANCIS BACON
> *"Of Atheism"*

The greatest devotion, greater than learning and
praying, consists in accepting the world
exactly as it happens to be.

> HASIDIC SAYING

She was made to realize once and for all that
this earth on which they lived turning about
in space did not revolve, as she had believed,
for the sake of little people.
"Not for big people either," she reminded the
boy when she saw his secret smile.

> MARY NORTON
> The Borrowers

54. Religion

Thou hast made us for Thyself, and the heart of man is
restless until it finds its rest in Thee.

> ST. AUGUSTINE
> Confessions

Even if God did not exist, religion would still
be holy and divine.

> CHARLES BAUDELAIRE

If God did not exist, it would be necessary to invent
him.

VOLTAIRE
"Epistle to the Author of the Three Imposters"

'Twas only fear first in the world made gods.

BEN JOHNSON
Sejanus

As one can ascend to the top of a house by means
of a ladder or a bamboo or a staircase or a rope,
so divers are the ways and means to approach
God, and every religion in the world shows one
of these ways.

RAMAKRISHNA

But everywhere there is, in addition to such practical
rationalism, a sense of something transcending the
expected or natural, a sense of the Extraordinary,
Mysterious, or Supernatural.

ROBERT H. LOWIE
Primitive Religion

Men despise religion; they hate it, and fear it is true.

BLAISE PASCAL
Pensées

What is your religion? I mean—not what you
know about religion but the belief that helps you most?

GEORGE ELIOT

In the beginning of days Wulbari and man lived close
together and Wulbari lay on top of Mother Earth,
Asase Ya. Thus it happened that, as there was so little

space to move about in, man annoyed the divinity, who
in disgust went away and rose up to the present place
where one can admire him but not reach him.

KRACHI FOLKTALE
in African Folktales and Sculpture *by Paul Radin*

The idea of Christ is much older than Christianity.

GEORGE SANTAYANA

Infidelity does not consist in believing or in
disbelieving: it consists in professing to believe
what one does not believe.

THOMAS PAINE
Age of Reason

There lives more faith in honest doubt,
Believe me, than in half the creeds.

ALFRED, LORD TENNYSON
"In Memoriam"

It is the way of those who follow the Judaeo-Christian
path to be troubled, to search the sky and their own
hearts for signs and portents that all is not well.

MARGARET MEAD
A Way of Seeing

A quiet conscience makes one so
serene!
Christians have burnt each other,
quite persuaded
That all the Apostles would have done
as they did.

LORD BYRON
Don Juan

When I mention religion, I mean the Christian religion;
and not only the Christian religion but the Protestant
religion; and not only the Protestant religion, but the
Church of England.

HENRY FIELDING
Tom Jones

We have just enough religion to make us hate,
but not enough to make us love one another.

JONATHAN SWIFT
Thoughts on Various Subjects

Religion is the sigh of the oppressed creature,
the feelings of a heartless world, just as it is
the spirit of unspiritual conditions. It is the
opium of the people.

KARL MARX
Introduction to a Critique of the
Hegelian Philosophy of Right

Prayer does not change God, but changes
him who prays.

SÖREN KIERKEGAARD

Prayers are no superstition, they are more
real than the acts of eating, drinking, sitting,
or walking.

MOHANDAS K. GANDHI

Priests and rituals are only crutches for the
crippled life of the soul.

FRANZ KAFKA

To have a positive religion is not necessary.
To be in harmony with yourself and the universe
is what counts, and this is possible without
positive and specific formulation in words.

JOHANN VON GOETHE

———————

I believe in an America that is officially neither
Catholic, Protestant or Jewish—where no public
official either requests or accepts instruction on public
policy from the Pope, the National Council of Churches,
or any other ecclesiastical source—where no religious
body seeks to impose its will directly or indirectly
upon the general populace or the public acts of its
officials—and where religious liberty is so indivisible
that an act against one church is treated as an act
against all.

... Finally, I believe in an America where religious
intolerance will someday end—where all men and
all churches are treated as equal—where every man
has the same right to attend or not to attend
the church of his choice—where there is no Catholic
vote, no anti-Catholic vote, no bloc voting of any
kind—and where Catholics, Protestants and Jews,
both the lay and the pastoral level, will refrain from
those attitudes of disdain and derision which have so
often marred their works in the past, and promote
instead the American ideal of brotherhood.

JOHN F. KENNEDY
Address to the Greater Houston Ministerial
Association, Houston, Texas, September 12, 1960

55. Hope

Man is, properly speaking, based upon Hope;
he has no other possession but Hope.

THOMAS CARLYLE
Sartor Resartus

Hope, deceitful as it is, serves at least to lead us to
the end of life along an agreeable road.

FRANÇOIS LA ROCHEFOUCAULD
Maxims

It is necessary to hope, though hope should always
be deluded; for hope itself is happiness, and its
frustrations, however frequent, are yet less dreadful
than its extinction.

SAMUEL JOHNSON
The Idler

We have no right to have no hope, because if we
have no hope, there is no hope. The basic ethics
for modern man conscious of what humanity is running
into is to firmly stick to the will of doing something
about it and therefore the belief that something
can be done about it.

JACQUES MONOD
The New York Times, *March 15, 1971*

Who can separate his faith from his actions, or his
belief from his occupations?

KAHLIL GIBRAN
The Prophet

———————

Dream and deed are not as different as many think.
All the deeds of men are dreams at first, and become
dreams in the end.

THEODORE HERZL
Postscripts, Altneuland

———————

When the Roman Stoic experienced catastrophes, he
took them with courage of resignation. But the typical
American, after he has lost the foundations of his
existence, works for new foundations.

PAUL TILLICH

———————

Work without Hope draws nectar in a sieve,
And Hope without an object cannot live.

SAMUEL TAYLOR COLERIDGE

———————

The miserable have no other medicine
But only hope.

WILLIAM SHAKESPEARE
Measure for Measure, *III:i*

———————

"One can't believe impossible things."
"I daresay you haven't had much practice," said
the Queen. "When I was your age, I always did it
for half an hour a day. Why, sometimes I've believed
as many as six impossible things before breakfast."

LEWIS CARROLL
Through The Looking Glass

Hope is the thing with feathers
That perches in the soul,
And sings the tune without the words,
And never stops at all.

EMILY DICKINSON

Every journey has an end—
When at the worst affairs will mend—
Dark the dawn when day is nigh—
Hustle your horse and don't say die!

WILLIAM S. GILBERT
Iolanthe

Receive what cheer you may:
The night is long that never finds the day.

WILLIAM SHAKESPEARE
Macbeth IV:3

And if this day is not a fulfilment of your needs and my love, then let it be a promise till another day.

KAHLIL GIBRAN
The Prophet

In spite of everything I still believe that people are really good at heart. I simply can't build up my hopes on a foundation consisting of confusion, misery, and death. I see the world gradually being turned into a wilderness, I hear the ever approaching thunder, which will destroy us too, I can feel the sufferings of millions and yet, if I look up into the heavens, I think that it will all come right, that this cruelty too will end, and that peace and tranquillity will return again.

ANNE FRANK
The Diary of a Young Girl

I wish to live because life has within it that which is good, that which is beautiful, and that which is love. Therefore, since I have known all of these things, I have found them to be reason enough and—I wish to live. Moreover, because this is so, I wish others to live for generations and generations and generations and generations.

LORRAINE HANSBERRY
in To Be Young, Gifted and Black

———

After all, life, for all its agonies of despair and loss and guilt, is exciting and beautiful, amusing and artful and endearing, full of liking and love, at times a poem and a high adventure, at times noble and at times very gay; and whatever (if anything) is to come after it—we shall not have this life again.

ROSE MACAULAY
The Towers of Trebizond

———

To live is like to love—all reason is against it, and all healthy instinct for it.

SAMUEL BUTLER
Notebooks

———

Be not afraid of life. Believe that life is worth living, and your belief will help create the fact.

WILLIAM JAMES

Selected Bibliography

Following are some of the books we have used that might be of interest for your further reference or reading:

Abrams, Charles. *The City Is the Frontier.* Harper & Row, 1965.

Bagdikian, Ben H. *In the Midst of Plenty: The Poor in America.* Beacon Press, 1964.

Boni, Margaret Bradford (ed.). *The Fireside Book of Favorite American Songs.* Simon and Schuster, 1952.

Boorstin, Daniel J. (ed.). *An American Primer.* Mentor, 1968.

Braude, Jacob M. (ed.). *Source Book for Speakers and Writers.* Prentice-Hall, 1968.

Clark, William R. *Explorers of the World.* Doubleday, 1968.

Filler, Louis (ed.). *The President Speaks, from McKinley to Lyndon Johnson.* Putnam (Capricorn Books), 1965.

Glazer, Nathan and Moynihan, Daniel Patrick. *Beyond the Melting Pot.* M.I.T. Press, 1963.

Hofstadter, Richard. *The American Political Tradition.* Alfred A. Knopf, 1967.

Jacobs, Jane. *The Death and Life of Great American Cities.* Random House, 1961.

Joseph, Franz M. (ed.). *As Others See Us, The United States Through Foreign Eyes.* Princeton University Press, 1959.

Kakonis, Tom E. and Wilcox, James C. (eds.). *Now and Tomorrow: The Rhetoric of Culture in Transition.* D. C. Heath and Co., 1971.

Kelen, Emory (ed.). *Fifty Voices of the Twentieth Century.* Lothrop, Lee and Shepard, 1970.

Kennedy, John F. *Profiles in Courage.* Harper & Row, 1956.

Kieran, John (ed.). *Treasury of Great Nature Writing*. Hanover House, 1957.

King, Martin Luther, Jr. *Why We Can't Wait*. Signet Books, 1963.

Lisitzky, Gene. *Four Ways of Being Human: An Introduction to Anthropology*. The Viking Press, 1956.

Luboff, Norman and Stracke, Win. *Songs of Man*. Prentice-Hall, 1965.

Marsh, Irving T. and Ehre, Edward (eds.). *Best of the Best Sports Stories*. E. P. Dutton and Co., 1964.

Milne, Lorus J. and Milne, Margery. *The Balance of Nature*. Alfred A. Knopf, 1960.

Mumford, Lewis. *The City in History*. Harcourt Brace Jovanovich, 1961.

Popenoe, David (ed.). *The Urban Industrial Frontier*. Rutgers University Press, 1969.

Prochnow, Herbert V. and Prochnow, Herbert V., Jr. *A Treasury of Humorous Quotations*. Harper & Row, 1969.

Rugoff, Milton (ed.). *The Great Travelers*. 2 Vols. Simon and Schuster, 1960.

Shapley, Harlow; Rapport, Samuel and Wright, Helen (eds.). *The New Treasury of Science*. Harper & Row, 1965.

Simpson, James B. (ed.). *Contemporary Quotations*. Thomas Y. Crowell, 1964.

Steinbeck, John. *America and Americans*. The Viking Press, 1966.

White, William S. *Citadel: The Story of the United States Senate*. Harper & Bros., 1956.

Wind, Herbert Warren (ed.). *The Realm of Sport*. Simon and Schuster, 1966.

Source Index with Biographical Notes

Heckscher, August (born 1913)
American civic official and social
critic, 20
Hemingway, Ernest (1899–1961)
American novelist, 237
Henry, Joseph (1797–1878)
American physicist; first director
of Smithsonian Institution, 1846–
1878, 223
Henry, Patrick (1736–1799)
American orator and revolutionary
leader, 55, 125
Heraclitus (6th–5th Century B.C.)
Greek philosopher, 128
Herrick, Robert (1591–1674)
English poet, 184
Herschberger, Ruth (born 1917)
American writer, 30
Herzl, Theodore (1860–1904)
Austrian journalist and founder of
Zionism, 292
Herzog, Maurice (born 1919)
French mountain climber and ex-
plorer, 229
Hesse, Hermann (1877–1962)
German-Swiss novelist, poet, es-
sayist, and literary critic, 39–40
Hillary, Sir Edmund (born 1919)
New Zealand mountain climber
and explorer; one of the first men
to reach the summit of Mount
Everest, 1953, 228
Hilton, James (1900–1954)
English novelist, 10
Hinckle, Warren (born 1938)
American editor and journalist,
197, 268
Hitler, Adolf (1889–1945)
German dictator and Chancellor,
1933–1945, 117
Hoffer, Eric (born 1902)
American longshoreman and es-
sayist, 7, 47, 122, 155, 176, 177,
183, 233
Hoffman, Abbie (born 1936)
American writer and political ac-
tivist, 17, 148
Hokusai (1760–1849)
Japanese painter, 51–52
Holiday, Billie (1915–1959)
Black American jazz singer, 233

Holmes, Oliver Wendell, Jr.
(1841–1935)
American jurist and writer; As-
sociate Justice, U.S. Supreme
Court, 1902–1932, 31, 48, 127, 201,
209, 267
Holt, John (contemporary)
American educator and writer,
219
Homer (850?–800? B.C.)
Greek epic poet, 87
Hopkins, Gerard Manley
(1844–1889)
English poet, 285
Hornaday, William Temple
(1854–1937)
American zoologist, 222, 249, 258,
259–60
Horwitz, Julius (born 1920)
American social worker and
writer, 21, 145, 146
Hottell, Major John Alexander
(died 1970)
American Army officer, 84
Housman, A. E. (1859–1936)
English classical scholar and poet,
185
Hubbard, Elbert (1856–1915)
American writer, editor, and
printer, 94
Hughes, Charles Evans (1862–1948)
American jurist; Chief Justice, U.S.
Supreme Court, 1930–1941, 127
Hughes, Everett (born 1897)
American sociologist, 151
Hughes, Langston (1902–1967)
Black American poet and writer,
20, 23, 104
Hugo, Victor (1802–1885)
French novelist, 12, 226
Hutchens, John K. (contemporary)
American writer, 238
Huxley, Aldous (1894–1963)
English novelist and essayist, 58,
72, 159
Huxley, Sir Julian (born 1887)
English biologist and writer, 176
Huxley, Thomas Henry (1825–1895)
English biologist, 225, 281
Huxtable, Ada Louise (born 1921)
American architecture critic and
journalist, 22

Koran
The sacred book of Islam, believed to have been revealed by God to the Prophet Mohammed, 211, 268, 280

Kostelanetz, André (born 1910)
American orchestra conductor, 5

Kostelanetz, Richard (born 1940)
American critic and cultural historian, 220

Krachi folktale, 287–88

Kramer, Jerry (born 1936)
American football player, 277

Kraus, Lili (born 1908?)
Austrian pianist, 208

Krutch, Joseph Wood (born 1893)
American educator, critic, and essayist, 164, 212, 226, 248, 251, 253, 258–59

La Farge, Oliver (1901–1963)
American ethnologist and novelist, 225

La Guardia, Fiorello (1882–1947)
American lawyer, congressman, and mayor of New York City, 1933–1945, 156

Lahr, Bert (1895–1967)
American comedian and actor, 267

Lang, Pearl (born 1922)
Black American ethnologist, dancer, and choreographer, 242

Lao-Tse (Lao-Tzu)
(c. 604 B.C.–c. 531 B.C.)
Chinese philosopher, 131

La Rochefoucauld, François, Duc de
(1613–1680)
French writer, 59, 128, 183, 291

Lawrence, D. H. (1885–1930)
English novelist, 262

Le Shan, Eda (contemporary)
American psychologist and writer, 27

Lee, Ann (1736–1784)
American religious mystic, founder of Shaker Society, 122

Leonard, George B. (born 1931)
American educator, 219

Leopold, Aldo (born 1913)
American educator, 251

Lerner, Max (born 1902)
American columnist, author, and educator, 29, 92

Lester, Julius (contemporary)
Black American essayist and critic, 101, 106

Levy, Amy (contemporary)
American schoolgirl, 67

Lewis, Oscar (1914–1971)
American anthropologist and writer, 146–47

Lewis, Sinclair (1885–1951)
American novelist and playwright, 95, 96, 99–100

Lincoln, Abraham (1809–1865)
Sixteenth President of the United States, 15, 18, 100, 107, 111, 112, 148

Lindbergh, Charles Augustus
(born 1902)
American aviator, 12–13

Lisitzky, Gene (contemporary)
American writer, 178

Livy (59 B.C.–A.D. 17)
Roman historian, 88, 119

Lloyd, Harold (1893–1971)
American film comedian, 268

Loden, Barbara (born 1937)
American actress and film-maker, 94

Lofting, Hugh (1886–1947)
Anglo-American writer and illustrator, 259, 261–62

London, Jack (1876–1916)
American novelist, 274

Longfellow, Henry Wadsworth
(1807–1882)
American poet, 39

Lowell, Amy (1874–1925)
American poet, 262

Lowell, James Russell (1819–1891)
American poet and essayist, 56, 67, 234

Lowie, Robert H. (1883–1957)
American anthropologist, 287

MacArthur, Douglas (1880–1964)
American general, 89, 90

Macaulay, Dame Rose (1881–1958)
English novelist, 294

Macaulay, Thomas Babington
(1800–1859)
English historian and statesman, 240

Machiavelli, Niccolò (1469–1527)

Ryan, Frank (born 1936)
American football player and mathematician, 273
Sainte-Beuve, Charles Augustin (1804–1869)
French poet and literary critic, 239
Saint-Exupéry, Antoine de (1900–1944)
French aviator and author, 3, 46
Salinger, J. D. (born 1919)
American novelist, 188, 237
Salk, Jonas (born 1914)
American physician and virologist; developer of vaccine against poliomyelitis, 234
Sandburg, Carl (1878–1967)
American poet and biographer, 22–23, 78, 86, 116, 131–32, 177–78, 257
Santayana, George (1863–1952)
American poet and philosopher, born in Spain, 71, 288
Sarc, Ömer Celâl (born 1901)
Turkish economist and administrator, 96
Saroyan, William (born 1908)
American playwright, 63
Sarris, Andrew (born 1928)
American film critic, 266–67
Sartre, Jean-Paul (born 1905)
French philosopher, playwright, and essayist, 123, 172, 186
Schlesinger, Arthur, Jr. (born 1917)
American historian, 78, 95, 157–58
Schnitzler, Arthur (1862–1931)
Austrian playwright and novelist, 196
Schopenhauer, Arthur (1788–1860)
German philosopher, 77, 139, 186, 201
Schulz, Charles M. (born 1922)
American comic-strip artist, 189
Schweitzer, Albert (1875–1965)
Alsatian musician, physician, and missionary in Africa; winner of Nobel Peace Prize, 1952, 196
Scott, George C. (born 1927)
American film actor, 244
Seldes, Gilbert (1893–1971)
American writer and critic, 265, 269
Sendak, Maurice (born 1928)

American illustrator and writer, 98
Seneca, Lucius Annaeus (4 B.C.?–A.D. 65)
Roman statesman and philosopher, 143, 200
Sennett, Mack (1884–1960)
American film director and producer, 269–70
Shakespeare, William (1564-1616)
English playwright and poet, 34, 38, 63, 67, 163, 170, 174–75, 183, 184, 194, 198, 200, 206, 254–55, 292, 293
Sharp, William (Fiona MacLeod) (1855–1905)
Scottish poet and man of letters, 203
Shaw, George Bernard (1856–1950)
English playwright and critic, 3, 6, 12, 14, 16, 18, 31, 33, 34, 37, 39, 44, 50, 51, 58, 72, 79, 88, 119, 120, 125, 136, 142, 147, 159, 163, 176, 210, 217, 219, 220, 233, 262
Shawn, Ted (1891–1972)
American dancer, 242
Shelley, Percy Bysshe (1792–1822)
English poet, 44, 60, 185, 282
Sherman, William Tecumseh (1820–1891)
American general, 88
Sillcox, Lewis Ketcham (born 1886)
American mechanical engineer, 248
Sinatra, Frank (born 1919)
American singer and actor, 244
Sinsheimer, Robert (born 1920)
American biophysicist, 177
Skinner, Cornelia Otis (born 1901)
American actress and writer, 34
Smith, Adam (1723–1790)
Scottish economist, 138
Smith, Alfred E. (1873–1944)
American political leader; governor of New York State, 160
Smith, Dennis (contemporary)
American writer and New York City fireman, 152
Smith, Logan Pearsall (1865–1946)
American essayist, 138, 148
Smith, Sydney (1771–1845)
English clergyman and author, 230

Snow, C. P. (born 1905)
English novelist and scientist, 161
Socrates (470?–399 B.C.)
Greek philosopher, 70
Solzhenitsyn, Aleksandr I.
(born 1918)
Russian novelist, Nobel Prize winner, 1970, 191, 209, 214–15, 232
Song of Solomon, 184
Songs. (See American, English, Irish . . .)
Spencer, Herbert (1820–1903)
English philosopher, 11, 123, 222
Spock, Benjamin (born 1903)
American physician and writer, 42, 45
Stanislavsky, Constantin Sergeyevich (1863–1938)
Russian actor, theatrical director, and drama teacher, 243
Stanley, Henry M. (1841–1904)
English explorer and writer, 231
Stanton, Elizabeth Cady
(1815–1902)
American social reformer and women's rights advocate, 129
Stark, Freya (born 1893)
English historian and travel writer, 35
Stein, Gertrude (1874–1946)
American poet and playwright, 239
Steinbeck, John (1902–1968)
American novelist, 98, 113
Steinberg, David (born 1942)
American comedian, 266
Stekel, Wilhelm (1868–1940)
Austrian psychiatrist, 206
Stendhal, Henri (1783–1842)
(pseudonym of Marie Henri Beyle)
French novelist and critic, 238
Stevenson, Adlai Ewing (1900–1965)
American statesman and diplomat, 86, 125, 126, 142, 154
Stevenson, Robert Louis (1850–1894)
Scottish novelist, essayist, and poet, 62
Stravinsky, Igor (1882–1971)
American composer, born in Russia, 208
Sumner, William Graham
(1840–1910)

American economist and sociologist, 117–18
Supreme Court, U.S., 104
Swahili proverb, 143
Swift, Jonathan (1667–1745)
English clergyman, satirist, and poet, 159, 163, 289
Swinburne, Algernon Charles
(1837–1909)
English poet, 171
Sypher, Wille (contemporary)
American writer and professor of English, 268
Syrus, See Publilius Syrus
Szent-Györgyi, Albert
(born 1893)
American biochemist, born in Hungary, 213, 223
Tacitus, Cornelius (c. 55 – c. 120)
Roman orator, politician, and historian, 77, 187
Talleyrand-Périgord, Charles Maurice
(1754–1838)
French statesman and writer, 160
Talmud
A compilation of Jewish oral law with commentaries and elaborations by rabbinical scholars, accepted as an authority by Orthodox Jews everywhere, 35, 38, 151, 152, 194, 196, 208, 284
Tatum, Jim (1913–1959)
American football coach, 272
Tawney, Richard H. (1880–1962)
English economist, 139–40
Taylor, Harold (born 1914)
American educator, 143
Taylor, James (born 1948)
American entertainer, 242, 281
Tennyson, Alfred, Lord (1809–1892)
English poet, 172, 288
Terrence (185–159 B.C.)
Roman playwright, 55, 121, 130
Thackeray, William Makepeace
(1811–1863)
English novelist, 28, 34, 202
Thant, U (born 1909)
Burmese statesman, Secretary General of the United Nations, 1962–1971, 71
Thomas, Dylan (1914–1953)
Welsh poet, 49, 171

311

Thoreau, Henry David (1817–1862) American naturalist and writer, 15, 17, 22, 48, 58, 118, 129, 140, 168, 198, 203, 247, 256

Thurber, James (1894–1961) American humorist and artist, 149

Tiger, Lionel (born 1937) American anthropologist, 27

Tillich, Paul (1888–1965) German Protestant theologian and philosopher, 292

Time essay, 196

Timothy, Book of, 136

Toffler, Alvin (born 1928) American writer, editor, and social commentator, 11, 224, 226

Tolstoy, Leo (1828–1910) Russian novelist and philosopher, 41, 86, 180, 235, 285

Travers, P. L. (born 1906) English writer, 40, 65, 171, 241

Trollope, Anthony (1815–1882) English novelist, 43

Truman, Harry S (1884–1972) Thirty-third President of the United States, 103, 109, 149, 158

Tunis, John R. (born 1889) American sportswriter, 272, 276

Tunney, Gene (born 1898) American boxer, 273

Turner, Frederick Jackson (1861–1932) American historian, 95

Twain, Mark (1835–1910) (pseudonym for Samuel Langhorne Clemens) American humorist and writer, 58, 116, 136, 195, 219

Twining, Nathan F. (born 1897) American Air Force general, 89

Udall, Stewart (born 1920) American lawyer and politician, 248–49

University of Iowa, 250

Van Goethem, Larry (contemporary) American journalist, 20

Van Gogh, Vincent (1853–1890) Dutch painter, 63, 285

Veblen, Thorstein (1857–1929) American economist, 272

Verdy, Violette (born 1931) French-born American ballerina, 243

Vidal, Gore (born 1925) American novelist and dramatist, 163

Vietnam War: GI, 84; Moratorium Day sign, 88

Vietnamese proverbs, 132, 211

Voltaire (1694–1778) (pseudonym for François Marie Arouet) French philosopher, playwright, and essayist, 77, 147, 201, 287

Wald, George (born 1906) American biologist and educator, 10, 246

Walker, James J. (1881–1946) American political leader, mayor of New York City, 1925–1932, 184

Wallace, William Ross (c. 1819–1881) American lawyer and poet, 34

Washington, George (1732–1799) First President of the United States, 109, 112, 157

Webb, Walter Prescott (1888–1963) American historian and educator, 75–76, 217, 218

Webster, Daniel (1782–1852) American lawyer, statesman, and orator, 93, 213

Weeks, Albert L. (contemporary) American professor and writer, 82

Welles, Orson (born 1915) American actor and film-maker, 264

Wells, Herbert George (H.G.) (1866–1946) English novelist and historian, 76

White, E. B. (born 1899) American essayist and novelist, 2, 17, 40, 71, 126, 169, 190–91, 218, 240, 283

White, Paul Dudley (born 1888) American physician, heart specialist, 49

White, T. H. (born 1906) British novelist, 260–61

White, William S. (born 1907) American political journalist and writer, 157, 260–61